Clark Smart Parents, Clark Smart Kids

ALSO BY CLARK HOWARD AND MARK MELTZER

Get Clark Smart!
Clark's Big Book of Bargains

Clark Howard & Mark Meltzer

Clark Smart

Teaching Kids

Parents,

of Every Age

Clark Smart

the Value of Money

Kids

New York

Library of Congress Cataloging-in-Publication Data

ISBN: 0-7868-8779-6

Hyperion books are available for special promotions and premiums. For details contact Michael Rentas, Assistant Director, Inventory Operations, Hyperion, 77 West 66th Street, 11th floor, New York, New York 10023, or call 212-456-0133.

FIRST EDITION

10   9   8   7   6   5   4   3   2   1

To Rebecca and Stephanie

with the hope that they

both become good people

and responsible adults

Contents

Acknowledgments

Writing this book was a special challenge, and I couldn't have done it without the guidance of a few very special people, chief among them my literary agent, Laurie Liss of Sterling Lord Literistic, and my editor, Mary Ellen O'Neill of Hyperion Publishing. When I needed direction, they were there to provide it.

I also want to thank Christa DiBiase, executive producer of my radio show, for her creativity and terrific research skills. Thanks also to Joni Alpert, her daughters Jaime and Lisa, and the entire staff of the *Clark Howard Show*, and to Fabia Wargin, of Creative Media Applications, Inc., who created and designed the terrific workbook section.

Two people who have taught me the most about what children need, and who teach me more every day, are my daughters, five-year-old Stephanie and fifteen-year-old Rebecca. You'll see a lot of them in these pages, as you will my wife, Lane, who keeps me going in the right direction.

Thanks also to people who shared their wisdom with me, including Michael Popkin and Jim Molis, whose ideas were invaluable.

A Note from Clark

Over the years I've had so many people thank me for the things they've learned from my syndicated radio show, my books, my TV reports, and my newspaper and magazine columns. Many have also asked me to help them teach their kids about money. That's what this book is about.

Too many children still think, as the old expression goes, that money grows on trees. And we, as parents, grandparents, aunts, and uncles, help create that impression by showering them with more and more stuff than any generation has ever had.

Some parents asked me to write a book for teenagers to read. But as I thought it through, I realized that parents really were asking for a way to communicate good money values to their children. They don't want their children to reach their twenties thinking there is an endless supply of money. I think it's cruel to teach that to a child, however inadvertently. When they learn the truth in adulthood, it's a tough process, with a lot of pain. It's far better for kids to understand more about money as they're growing up.

Kids may act like they're tuning us out, but they're learning our values even as they roll their eyes. Pick a high school senior, and he might be completely clueless about how to handle money or destined to be financially secure throughout life. It's part of what children learn, either accidentally or on purpose, from Mom and Dad. They watch what we do and learn from our mistakes and successes.

I got a call from an eighteen-year-old who for some reason had to take a year off between high school and college. He was living at home and working full-time, and told me he was able to save 75 percent of what he made. He wanted to know what he should do with the money. We talked about the Roth IRA, into which he could put $4,000 a year, to grow tax-free until he retires. I asked if he would have any money left over, and he said he'd have another $15,000. So I told him he'd need some of that for college, and he said the $15,000 was *after* he'd set aside money for college. How impressive is that? So I talked with him about doing a tax-managed portfolio, in which he could invest without having a lot of tax consequences.

This young man knew almost nothing about investments but had a great attitude about money—he believed that he should depend only on himself to save money. He said his dad had talked with him about money for as long as he could remember, and that's how he came to have such great money values.

My wife, Lane, grew up in a very suc-cessful family. Her father was a doctor, one of her brothers is a doctor, and another is a lawyer, and Lane has had wonderful success as an actress. But one thing that amazed me when I became a member of her family is that they never talked about money. So Lane and her siblings reached adulthood and didn't have the first idea about how to handle money. It's not just how you use your money—it's how you communicate about money to your kids.

Some people think there's something wrong with talking to their children about money—about how much they earn or how much things cost. I hear again and again that parents would rather talk to their children about "the birds and the bees" than about money. But you have to get past that, because, just as you don't want your kids to learn certain kinds of information from the kids at the playground or the mall, they need to learn about money from you.

Tell your kids why and how you make financial decisions—what you do to stretch a dollar, how you save money out of each paycheck. They'll learn from what you tell them and how you coach them. Some parents want schools to teach those things, but you are the best teacher your child is ever going to have. You can be a great teacher, and a great leader, to your child.

It's also important to be consistent with your message. Lane says I'm sometimes inconsistent, because I love bargains so much that I'll often buy things for my daughters, Rebecca and Stephanie, or for Lane just because they're a great deal. I have a certain lack of discipline that communicates a bad message. Even as I'm teaching my teenager, Rebecca, not to overpay for something, I'm inadvertently teaching her to overspend. Getting a great deal is terrific, but sometimes not spending the money is even better. If you're not careful about how much you spend, you can go broke saving money.

What you teach your children about money depends on their ages. You can start early, but the techniques you use with a four-year-old are different from those you use with a fourteen-year-old. In *Clark Smart Parents, Clark Smart Kids*, I've created sections devoted to children (up to age eleven); teenagers (including college-age children); and adult children—the twenty-something kids who aren't quite fully independent adults. In the final section, you'll see another aspect of the parent-child dialogue about money. This time, you are the child, and I have advice about how to talk to your parents about their finances.

I hope this book helps you teach your kids to become more "Clark Smart."

Clark Howard

Clark Smart Parents, Clark Smart Kids

CHAPTER 1

Kids

Teaching young children about money produces a trifecta of benefits: It helps them in school, it helps them with values, and it helps you save money.

Elementary schoolchildren learn how to add and subtract, and you can bring that alive for them with the suggestions you'll see in this section about ways that they can save you money, and they become part of the team in helping you save. You'll see that, with things you do every day and every week, there are steps you can involve your child in that will give him or her a stake in the game.

Parents ask me, "When is my child old enough to start talking about money?" The reality is there isn't one day, one age, or one stage; it's a process and we learn it piece by piece. I don't want you to make your children money-obsessed, and I don't want you to be money-obsessed. But know that each time a child asks you to buy something, there's an opportunity for you to teach the cost of things, and the value of them. When children are about four, you can begin, gently, to teach the concept, and not just by saying no. You might allow a child to have not what they want, but something else that's cheaper, or to have what they want in a few months. When I tell my five-year-old, Stephanie, that we can't buy something, she says, "Is it not a-faw-dable?" It's not enough to tell a young child she can't have something. It's more important to explain why. That doesn't mean children are little adults. They're not, and they are there to be shaped and molded with our values. That's one of our responsibilities as parents—guiding our children. And sometimes with children, you don't ask them, you tell them. But over time, this is a lesson you can teach them. If you communicate good values over time, your children will learn them.

✳ It Starts with You ✳

You thought you were buying a book about your kids, but before we get to that, it's important to deal with your money personality. Are you a saver? Or are you a spender? It's vital for you to know your own habits, so you don't say one thing to your kids and do another. They'll learn more from what they see you do than from what you say.

To help figure out your money personality, I've created a simple quiz that covers some of the basic areas of spending and saving.

Taking this quiz may teach you some things about the way you handle money that will make a difference in what you do going forward, as well as how best to communicate with your child. If you're reading this book with your spouse, take the quiz and have your spouse take it separately. It may generate conversation between you. If you have an ex-spouse, talk to him or her about how you can instill values in your kids even when you are living apart. If you have an amicable relationship, you may be able to create some joint goals and work together to achieve them.

It helps to know your child's money personality as well, if he has developed one yet. Is he generally responsible? Is he eager to spend? To save? Does he like to share? Does he show off his money to other kids? Does he play the big spender? Is he a hoarder?

The answers to all of these questions will help you make good decisions about how to help your child develop good money values. But don't overanalyze your child. At this age, kids are clay, and you can mold them over the years into the right shape.

What's Your Money Personality?

1. Before you get your paycheck, how much money do you save in an employer-sponsored retirement plan or SEP if you're self-employed?

   A. I put 15 percent (or the maximum my employer allows) into my employer's plan
   B. I put 10–14 percent into my employer's plan
   C. I put 5–9 percent into my employer's plan
   D. I put 1–5 percent into my employer's plan
   E. I don't put any money aside in my employer's plan

2. How much money do you put in a traditional IRA or Roth IRA per year?

   A. I max out my IRA plan each year
   B. I put $3,000 in my plan each year
   C. I put $2,000 in my plan each year
   D. I put $1,000 in my plan each year
   E. I don't contribute to an IRA

3. How much money do you have in a rainy-day account?

   A. I have enough to cover six months to a year of living expenses
   B. I have enough to cover three to six months of living expenses
   C. I have enough to cover one to three months of living expenses
   D. I don't have any money in savings

4. If you own a home, how does the balance on your mortgage compare to the value of your house?

   A. I don't have a mortgage—I own my home
   B. The balance on my mortgage is much less than the value of my home
   C. The balance on my mortgage is less but close to the value of my home
   D. The balance on my mortgage is more than the value of my home

5. If you own a car, do you own your car free and clear or do you have a loan?

   A. I don't have a car loan
   B. I have one year left
   C. I have two to four years left
   D. I have four to seven years left

6. Let's look at your credit card balances

    A. I pay my cards off in full each month
    B. I carry a balance but pay more than the minimum each month
    C. I pay only the minimum each month
    D. I have trouble making minimum payments each month

7. When purchasing electronics, furniture, and appliances, I usually

    A. wait until I have the cash and then buy the item and pay in full
    B. put the item on a credit card and pay it off in a couple of months
    C. buy the item on "buy now, pay later" or "no down payment, no payments, no interest" plans because I can't afford what I want right away
    D. put the items on a credit card without a plan to pay them off

SCORING

For questions 1 and 2, give yourself 20 points for an "A," 15 points for a "B," 10 points for a "C," 5 points for a "D," and 0 points for an "E."

For questions 3–7, give yourself 12 points for an "A," 8 points for a "B," 4 points for a "C," and 0 points for a "D."

How did you do?

80–100 points: Congratulations—you should have written this book! You are a saver for sure. Some might even call you a miser, but I call you Clark Smart.

55–79 points: You have developed some great saving habits. Keep it up and consider aiming even higher.

41–54 points: You are making efforts to save, but you can do better. Try to increase your savings and decrease what you owe each year, and you'll see your score shoot up.

30–40 points: We need to have a talk.

Less than 30 points: Like in the game Monopoly, you need to go to jail and read *Get Clark Smart* before you go any further.

Now that you've taken the money personality quiz, I'd like you to come up with a list of at least three goals for both yourself and your children that you will work on as you read this book.

For example, one of your goals might be to increase your retirement savings to 10 percent of your annual pay. You might choose to work on paying off your car loan in eighteen months. Or you might elect to bring your lunch to work, and put the money you save each month into a mutual fund.

Next, write down some goals for your child. For example,

○ teach him why it matters to save money,

○ help him start a retirement account with the money he earns in his summer job,

○ get him to start saving to help pay for his prom.

✳ The Clark Smart Allowance Plan for Kids ✳

You should start giving your child an allowance as soon as he or she is old enough to understand the concept of chores. That's around first grade for most children.

The concept behind my allowance plan is that children should have a basic set of responsibilities and get a basic allowance, which goes up as the child gets older. Then, just as you might earn a bonus at your job for doing more, you should allow your child to earn bonus money by doing extra chores.

In my plan, children get $1 a week in allowance for each grade level. So a first-grader gets $1 a week and a fourth-grader gets $4 a week. That's the base pay, which a child earns by doing a few basic chores—making her bed each day, putting her dirty clothes in the hamper, putting away her toys, and loading the dishwasher or washing dishes.

My five-year-old, Stephanie, already knows how to clean the kitchen floor. She actually enjoys it, and she's good at it, because we have one of those Swiffer

• Your Goals •

_____

_____

_____

_____

_____

_____

_____

_____

_____

_____

_____

_____

_____

_____

_____

_____

_____

_____

• Your Child's Goals •

_____

_____

_____

_____

_____

_____

_____

_____

_____

_____

_____

_____

_____

_____

_____

_____

_____

_____

cleaners, and she likes using it. I think that's important, because if a child dislikes every chore, then it becomes a battle. Stephanie also sets the table, because that's an easy responsibility for a young child. She's still having a little trouble figuring out where everything goes, but she gets the napkins and plates out there. The repetition teaches her that she has responsibilities.

Next, the child and other family members share a few of the other household tasks, which rotate each week. We assign those chores with a "chore wheel." Every week we spin it, and Stephanie gets different tasks. It might be taking out the trash, feeding the dogs, or putting away groceries. We don't include mopping, because that could lead to a child's slipping and falling, or being around dangerous chemicals.

Kids don't get extra allowance money for doing chore wheel tasks. These are things that everyone in the house shares, and doing them teaches them that everyone has a role in keeping the house running. The variety allows them to do new things and keeps them from becoming drudgery.

Finally, there are bonus chores, which

give kids a chance to earn more, perhaps 25 cents to $2 more, depending on the chore. These are the kinds of things you might have to pay somebody to do—so why not let your child earn money doing them? If your child helps you make lunches for the rest of the family, that's worth an extra 25 cents. If he vacuums the carpet or dusts the furniture, that's good for 50 cents more. Raking leaves or cleaning windows is good for $1, and washing Mom's or Dad's car or shoveling snow from the driveway is good for $2.

You can pay more or less if $1 per grade level seems too high or low for your income level or where you live. Then, at the start of each school year, the child's allowance goes up $1—or whatever increment you have chosen—a week. It softens the blow of the end of summer vacation.

One way to figure out a good level of allowance to give your child is to ask other parents in your neighborhood what they give their children. That will give you an idea of what is common for kids their age and what the norm is in your area. Across the United States, the average allowance is $6 a week for six- to eight-year-olds, and $8 a week for kids nine to eleven, according to the *Wall Street Journal*.

If your child fails to do his basic chores each week, he doesn't get the week's allowance.

We also have a punishment system if Stephanie doesn't clean up her own room. If she doesn't put a toy away, it goes into the "No-no" room, which means she can't play with it for a week. That might make me seem like a cruel guy, but it has worked well. At the appropriate ages, you should continually teach logical consequences of behavior, good and bad. If you don't teach logical consequences, kids won't learn about their limits and boundaries.

I've taught Stephanie the value of a dollar by connecting it to something every child loves—toys. She loves little toys and trinkets, so I have her conditioned that the dollar store is the toy store. I give her a dollar and she knows that she can use it to pick out any item she wants at the toy store. I cover the tax.

Stephanie knows what she can get with the dollars she earns from her allowances or receives as gifts. Her grandmother gave her two dollar bills for her birthday, and she knew that meant she could get two toys at the dollar store. She didn't want to go anywhere else. We went with her and watched as she went through the store figuring out what she was going to buy. She started with a pile of things, then gradually put back items, one at a time, until she had narrowed it to three. She was really struggling with which one of the last three to eliminate. I could have just bought her the third one, but I didn't, and she was okay with that. Priorities are a hard thing to teach adults, and it's great to learn about them as early as possible. You should continue to instill the value of setting priorities—what is most valuable or important to you. Stephanie is five and she's got it.

I don't recommend giving young children an allowance to pay for school lunches. Pay that yourself and let the kids spend their money on the stuff they normally spend it on—video games, candy, ice cream, and toys. When your child reaches middle school or junior high— sixth, seventh, or eighth grade—an allowance should include more things. Kids are old enough at that point to learn the concept of budgeting. You give them the money for the week on Sunday, and they have to make sure they have enough for lunch come Friday, and don't blow it at the snack bar. At that point, it's $6 for sixth grade, plus whatever school lunch costs. If your child chooses to make lunch at home, give him a chance to benefit financially from that choice. Let's say school lunch costs $10 a week. Give your sixth-grader $6, plus $10 for school lunch. If he makes his lunch at home, let him pay you 50 cents a day for the ingredients, but let him keep the rest of the $10. You're teaching him the value of labor, and of bringing your own lunch, a habit that will benefit him greatly as an adult.

✳ The Clark Smart Allowance Plan for Kids ✳

• How Much to Pay •

First grade:	$1 a week
Second grade:	$2 a week
Third grade:	$3 a week
Fourth grade:	$4 a week
Fifth grade:	$5 a week
Sixth grade:	$6 a week
Seventh grade:	$7 a week
Eighth grade:	$8 a week

• Basic Chores •

Make the bed
Put dirty clothes in the hamper
Put away toys
Load dishwasher or wash dishes
Set the table

• Rotating Family Chores (the Chore Wheel) •

Feed pets
Take out the garbage
Put away groceries

• Bonus chores •

Make lunches for the family	25 cents per time
Dust furniture	50 cents per time
Vacuum carpet	50 cents per time
Rake leaves	$1 per time
Clean windows	$1 per time
Wash parents' car	$2 per time
Shovel snow from driveway	$2 per time

✳ Learning About Prices ✳

Teaching your children to be Clark Smart consumers means making your points over many years, and it's best to start early. You can't tell a fourth-grader what you make and where all the money goes. But you can teach her something about prices.

When my daughter Rebecca was in second and third grade, I started teaching her how to read price tags in stores. The supermarket is the easiest place to do that with a child, because even very young kids can easily relate to the idea of shopping for food. So that's a great opportunity to help teach your child how much things cost. With a very young child, you can start with basic price tags—this item costs one dollar and this item costs two dollars.

I taught Rebecca to read the shelf price tags that show how much each product costs per ounce. As she learned, she would point out that the store brand cost a certain amount per ounce, and the name brand cost a certain amount more. I used that as a way to teach her about the idea of relative value—the concept of how much money it takes to buy different things.

Unit pricing is important. We assume that the extra-large box is going to be cheaper per ounce than the regular-size box, but often that is not true. The food industry learned that people buy the big box because they want more of the item, not because they're worried about the price. So in many food product categories, the regular-size box is cheaper per ounce than the extra-large box. Many adults don't realize that, because they don't know how to read those unit-price labels, or don't bother. For example, many adults probably don't know that at least one toilet-paper manufacturer sells four rolls for 99 cents at many different kinds of stores, but all the packages are priced differently. That's because the four-packs at the more expensive stores have fewer sheets of toilet paper, whereas the ones sold at the discount stores have more sheets. If you check the shelf tags, you'll see the difference in the unit price. The packages with more sheets have a lower price per sheet.

If you show a child how to read the unit-price tag, and ingrain in him why it's important, he can use that skill for the rest of his life. Reading the shelf tags is also a good math exercise. Your child not only will have better money values, but will also do better in math class.

Explaining the concept of a "sale" is great for elementary school kids. One time you walk into the store a product costs $1.50 and another time you walk in and it's only $1. The way I explain it is that when a company has a new product out, and people who run the company want you to try it, they will offer you a better deal to encourage you to buy it. Or sometimes they're just not selling enough of an item, so they cut the price temporarily to boost sales.

One of the biggest challenges in teaching children about prices and value is that we don't use paper money much anymore. By using credit and debit cards so much, we've taught our children that you don't need real money to buy things, or when you do need money, you just go to the ATM and money comes out. It's difficult enough for adults to understand that just because they have a $5,000 credit limit on a credit card, they can't just pull it out and use it whenever they want. How do you explain to a child that plastic is not an unlimited source of money? I'll address that further in the "Teens" chapter. But with young kids, the best solution is to keep the cards in your wallet and, at least for a while, stick to cash. By the time they're in elementary school, children can count. So when you get to the register at the store, take out your money and count it while your child watches. Or have the child count it out. Stick with ones, fives, and tens to make it easier. That makes the message clear—food costs money and there is a limited amount of it.

If you use cash, you can set an amount you're willing to spend that day, and talk with your child about whether you have enough money to buy everything in your cart. Bring an inexpensive calculator with you, and let your kid add up the price of each item. I realize it's going to take longer to finish your shopping trip, but it's worth it if you can teach your child to be a smarter consumer. If the groceries add up to $52 and you have $40 in cash with you, you and your child can decide to put a few items back so you can stay within your $40 budget. The idea is to create a sense of limits, and not in a negative way, but in a positive way. If the Pop-Tarts cost $2 but the store brand is 99 cents, it's easy to show that buying the store brand instead will shave $1 off your grocery bill, and help you get back under budget.

Food coupons are another way to explain relative value, and it's easy to get your child motivated to help you with that. Tell your child if he clips and sorts the food coupons in the Sunday newspaper, you'll give him 25 cents out of every dollar you save. Some parents think of this as bribery, but to me it's fundamental capitalism. Few kids (or adults) will do something out of pure altruism—they want to see a tangible result of their efforts. Investors want to see a return on their money, or they have no incentive to continue investing. If your child becomes good enough at helping you save money on your grocery bill, why not give him some of the money? You win and your child learns the value of saving a buck.

Use the limits of your budget as a tool to get a child away from his fixation on name brands, which is fed by TV advertising. Kids believe everything they see on TV, and they need to learn that products aren't always as wonderful as the advertisement says, or worth the high price. My youngest daughter is five, too young to teach her this. But you can teach a child of seven or eight about advertising and breakfast cereals. Try this: If your child wants to buy a $3 box of Cap'n Crunch and there's a store brand of cereal that costs $1, tell her she can buy either—but you'll give her 50 cents (of the $2 savings) if she chooses to buy the store brand. She might still want the Cap'n Crunch, but she might also want the 50 cents. You're setting up a choice between the perceived value of an item and the value of money that goes in your pocket.

✳ Games for Kids ✳

Playing games with your children can help you teach them money concepts. With little children, it can be as simple as showing them different coins and paper money, and asking them which is worth more. As a prize, give them M&M's or crayons, currency they really value.

You can also teach your children the rewards of delayed gratification—saving for a goal (and earning interest on those savings) rather than getting it now—and build a value that will serve your child well throughout her life. Here's one way to do that. Get five finger puppets (or any small toy), and let your child play with one of them. After a little while, have her put the finger puppet in the "bank" (a shoe box or some other "home"). The next day, tell her that because she left the finger puppet in the bank, there are now two finger puppets in there. When she opens the lid, she will be very glad to see that her puppet now has a friend. After that play session, tell her that if she leaves the finger puppets in the bank for three days, then there will be even more of them. But if she takes them out and plays with them before the three days are up, they won't multiply and there still will be two. If she is able to wait, she will get a wonderful surprise when there are five puppets in the box at the end of the week.

In the 1960s, Stanford psychologist Walter Mischel found that young people who could delay gratification did better socially and academically in later life.

In the classic "Marshmallow Test," Dr. Mischel gave four-year-old nursery school students the option of receiving one marshmallow immediately or waiting until Dr. Mischel got back from running an errand of about fifteen minutes and receiving two marshmallows. One third of the tots grabbed their one marshmallow the instant Dr. Mischel left the nursery.

Dr. Mischel revisited the same subjects at age eighteen and found that those who had delayed gratification in the marshmallow test were socially and academically ahead of those who had immediately consumed their marshmallows. Those who had delayed gratification were more self-reliant and assertive, and better able to handle stress and frustration. They embraced challenges, took initiative, and persisted when faced with setbacks. They tested an average of 100 points higher on both verbal and math parts of the Scholastic Aptitude Test. In contrast, those who had not delayed gratification as children tended to be stubborn, indecisive, shy, envious, and angry teenagers. And they still did not postpone pleasure.

The next time you're wracked with guilt for saying "no" to your kids, remember that you're only doing it for their own good.

Here are some more ideas for elementary school kids:

1. Collect coins with the kids, and use what you find to contribute to a family treat at the end of the year, such as a day at an amusement park. Kids can help search for coins on the floor, under beds, and under sofa cushions. Display the money you find in big, clear containers, separated by type of coin.

2. Have the kids make their own birthday cards for friends and family, decorating them with art supplies and pictures from home. Put the money saved by not buying cards at the store into your amusement park fund. Ask the kids if they can think of other ways to save money for the special day. (Family members can put their change every day into several clear containers.)

3. Play "What item costs less?" Show your children pairs of items with price tags and ask which costs less, the $1.99 item or the $2.99 item. (For older kids, use shelf tags with unit price per ounce or per sheet of paper towel, and ask which is the better value.)

4. There's nothing better than a good old-fashioned lemonade stand. Kids can sell baked goods as well. Just make sure they have to pay for the ingredients and supplies. One mother even charged her kids rent for the space. It's a great way for them to learn how hard it can be to make money, and about net proceeds from sales.

   There's a great Web site, www.lemonadegame.com, that takes you through exactly what happens when you set up a lemonade stand, step-by-step: How much money you're going to make, what inventory you're going to need (lemons, cups, sugar, ice), and what the inventory is going to cost. It's a great way for elementary school kids to learn how to build a simple business plan.

Here are some other Web sites with games and great places for your child to have some fun and learn about money.

www.sesamestreet.com

Sesame Street's Web site has a neat Game Room, where your young child can learn how to count, an essential skill when handling money. As soon as you think your child is ready, you can start on this. They're always adding new games. When I looked, there was one in which Mr. Noodle wants to walk five dogs. Elmo tells your child to click on each dog he can find on the screen until he reaches five. If he clicks on another animal, like a walrus or a squirrel, it says something funny. It's a fantastic game to teach your child about numbers.

www.usmint.gov/kids

This site has a bunch of neat games that teach kids everything they would want to know about coins. You can color a quarter or take a "time machine" to solve coin mysteries.

www.moneyfactory.com/kids/start.html

The Bureau of Engraving and Printing has created a site full of games for kids, all about its favorite subject—money. (Incidentally, it teaches your kid that counterfeiters get caught!)

www.fleetkids.com

This is a cute Web site with a number of games to teach children about money, businesses, buying and selling, and how to make change. The games are similar to video games, which makes them perfect for older elementary school kids. The children won't get bored, and while they're playing the games, they'll learn money concepts, such as profit and loss and saving money.

✳ Affluenza ✳

We have so much more stuff than our parents had, and so do our children.

When I was a child, I'd get one pair of shoes when the school year started. My coauthor remembers getting a Scrabble game for his tenth birthday. Not a half dozen gifts, but one gift, and he was thrilled with it.

Today, that kind of appreciation for things is more rare, but it still exists. If your child doesn't ask you for every toy on the shelf, congratulations, and keep doing what you're doing. You've countered the impact of advertising and peer pressure. You can skip the rest of this section and move on to the next.

But even if your child does have "affluenza," a lack of appreciation for what we have that is brought on by abundance, I have some ideas you can use to help counteract it. One is to replace the old with the new. If your child wants a new toy, no problem. But he has to choose an old toy to give to charity. If he gets new clothes, some of the old clothes go to needy children. You'll teach your child the importance of helping people in need, and of appreciating what you have.

That's a great thing to try during the holidays. Have your kids choose a letter to Santa and buy a gift for a needy child. Each year, we do something called Christmas Kids, when my radio station collects gifts from the public for children who are in foster care. People pick a child to help, and they buy him or her two gifts. Each year, the foster children write thank-you notes to Santa, and it's easy to see how precious these gifts are to them. By contrast, my coauthor used to get annoyed at Christmas at the way his grandchildren would tear through a pile of holiday gifts. They'd rip open one great gift, look at it briefly, then throw it aside and rush to open the next gift. Instead of treasuring each gift, they ignored most of them. Getting twenty gifts diminished each one. It taught the kids not to value what they received. And it could teach them to place less value on each dollar that they spend.

You can use the holiday giving technique during the year as well, for birthdays or other occasions. Buy your child half as many gifts, and buy some for charity, and you'll be doing good for your child and many others. It will be a great experience for your child, a privilege for him or her to do something for another child.

You can also counter affluenza with an allowance. As I discussed in the Clark Smart Allowance Plan for kids, you should give a child $1 a week in allowance for each grade level. So a fourth-grader gets $4 a week in allowance. If your fourth-grader really wants a toy he's seen on TV, you don't have to tell him he can't have it. You can tell him to buy it with his allowance. When your child saves up enough money from his allowance, he can buy the toy. That gives you another opportunity to teach, because you can go through the weekly sale flyers and show your child how to buy the toy he wants for less money. You're teaching delayed gratification—saving for something you want—and you're teaching about pricing. Kids appreciate something so much more when they have to save up to buy it. It's empowering.

Or you can stop the I-want-itis by requiring your child to pay half when he wants a new toy. This is a great suggestion that I got from a woman at a taping for one of my TV specials. When her kids want a toy, they have to pay half the price with money from their allowances or from doing extra chores. That forces them to decide how important the toy really is. They have to set priorities as to what they want. The woman told me this is working fantastically for her, because the kids have a stake in the game, and she doesn't have to say no all the time.

That works well for toys, but clothes are a little different. You have to buy your child school clothes, but you don't have to buy everything he or she wants. I recommend you set a seasonal budget for clothes for your child, maybe $150 four times a year. Maybe more, maybe less, depending on what you can afford and what seems right to you. And that's the budget. If your eleven-year-old wants an outfit that will bust the clothing budget, she can buy that outfit out of her allowance.

Another way to restore a sense of limits, to yourself and your child, is to get back to using cash. There's something in our natures that makes it harder to spend real cash. Taking five twenties out of your wallet is more painful than pulling out your Visa card. If you have $50 or $100 in your wallet and after three or four days you're down to $15, you have a sense of how much you've spent and realize that you should conserve more. If you put $35 or $85 on your debit or credit card, you wouldn't have the same sense that your short-term resources are somewhat depleted. And if you don't have much cash in your wallet, you can honestly tell your child you don't have enough money right now to buy something she wants.

One of the major causes of affluenza is falling prices. Consumer goods—clothing, shoes, toys, and electronics—are much cheaper than they used to be relative to our incomes. My five-year-old knows that she can buy a toy for a dollar at the dollar store. But when I was a kid, you couldn't buy a toy for what's basically throwaway money.

This dramatic change is primarily a result of overseas manufacturing, which has made all kinds of goods much cheaper. When I was a kid, all shoes for sale here were made in this country. Today, practically none are made here. Today's children, even those who aren't from affluent families, can have multiple pairs of shoes. They can have designer shoes, or athletic shoes with flashing lights, and they all cost less than $10. The downside is the precious nature of what we buy is gone, and buying has become a lot more casual. Children pick that up from us.

As a parent, you're not doing your kids a favor if you let them partake of all that they want. If you buy them their fourteenth pair of jeans, you teach them there are no limits, a bad lesson it may take years to undo.

My radio producer Christa DiBiase at one time was embarrassed at how many shoes she'd bought that she barely ever wore. When she bought a new house, she showed me proudly how she had just a small section in the house for the shoes she had left. She'd gotten rid of the others and learned to place limits on herself. Over your lifetime, less is more.

✳ Birthday Parties and Other Celebrations ✳

Some parents have taken children's birthday parties a little too far. We get party invitations all the time from Stephanie's friends at school. I'm certain they cost more than a lot of people spend on wedding invitations. A clerk at a party store told us that many people get customized invitations at $5 per invitation. That's incredible.

Parents literally spend thousands of dollars to put on some of the birthday parties Stephanie attends. One person set up an amusement park in the community park, which included a real train kids could ride in that went around the park and a giant blow-up slide that kids could climb and slide down. This was for a three-year-old.

I know parents love their kids, but I just don't believe in that kind of excess. You can give your child a wonderful birthday party without spending large amounts of money.

For example, instead of getting a beautiful giant birthday cake in the shape of a llama or a hot cartoon character, bake a cake, or cupcakes, with your child. Stephanie loves to help Lane make birthday cupcakes, and she enjoys them so much more than when we buy them at the supermarket. She takes pride in having helped make them. And it saves so much money.

Here are some money-saving ideas:

1. Have a friend or relative dress up as a clown or other character your child enjoys. Maybe have him do magic tricks or play music. A magician can cost $300 or more per party.

2. Have your child help create invitations for his or her friends.

3. Have the kids run races instead of renting expensive rides.

Web sites to consult for more ideas:

www.kidspartyfun.com	*(See different ideas for themes and how to save big bucks on your child's big day)*
www.parents.com	*(See the section called "birthdays" for some great party ideas)*
www.birthdayexpress.com	*(Lots of great ideas and recipes for creative cakes and cupcakes)*

Top Tips for Kids

○ Determine your own money personality so your message to your kids matches your actions.

○ Give children $1 a week in allowance for each grade level.

○ Kids should earn their allowances by doing basic chores. Let them earn more by doing extra chores.

○ When you shop with your children, keep your credit cards in your wallet and stick to cash.

○ Have your child clip food coupons from the Sunday newspaper and give him 25 cents out of every dollar you save.

○ Give your daughter the choice of buying the $3 box of cereal or the $1 store brand, giving her 50 cents (of the $2 savings) if she chooses to buy the store brand.

○ Play money games with your kids to help teach them money concepts.

○ If your child wants a new toy or new clothes, tell him he has to choose an old toy to give to charity.

○ Counter I-want-it disease by making your child pay for half the cost of a toy with his allowance.

○ Buy your child half as many gifts as you normally do, and use the extra money to buy some for charity.

CHAPTER 2

Teens

In this chapter of *Clark Smart Parents, Clark Smart Kids,* I have some great ideas about how you can teach good money values to your teenager. But keep in mind that each teenager is different, and you have to do what works with yours. Some of my suggestions will flip on the little lightbulb above your head, and you'll think, "I never thought about that." With others, you'll wonder what planet I'm on that I would suggest something like that. That's because teenagers, at this unusual transitional stage in their lives, are so different.

I've worked very hard to instill values in my daughters. I've told my teenager over and over that, when she's an adult, she is the one who is going to have to make choices about money. I often read suggestions from other experts and ask Rebecca what she thinks of them, using them as a way to engage her and to continue to build the concept that money is in limited supply, and that you have to think about how to use it.

We all remember from our own teenage years what an awkward time it is. Sometimes teens feel like adults; other times they feel like children. They may have the outward sophistication of adults, but the inward immaturity of children. So even when your teen is rolling his eyes at you as you talk about something, he is listening, and wants to hear what you're saying. The only time your teen will really tune you out is when he sees total hypocrisy—when you tell him to do one thing but he knows you're doing another. That's why you'll see a theme, especially in this "Teens" chapter, that you should walk the walk as well as talk the talk if you expect your teen to absorb these values.

Kids' money values are not monolithic. You may have a teen who's so responsible that she could teach you a thing or two about money values. But she may not have the tools to put those values to work. That's what I hope you take away from this chapter—information to guide your teen and nurture her interest. I'll share some ideas on teaching your teen about where your family fits in the financial universe, credit and credit cards, working and saving, cars, investing, and scams.

✳ The Clark Smart Allowance Plan for Teens ✳

As I said in the section on allowances for younger children (The Clark Smart Allowance Plan for Kids), I believe you should give a child $1 a week for each grade the child reaches in school, and add $1 each year. So a ninth-grader gets $9 a week and a tenth-grader gets $10 a week.

Teens shouldn't get that allowance just for breathing—it comes with responsibilities as well. You decide what minimum responsibilities your teenager should have. But I recommend you start with requiring a teen to keep his room clean, make his bed every day, and do at least one family or household chore a week to earn his allowance. If he doesn't do those things, then that week he gets no allowance. Allowance is a privilege, not an automatic right.

Behavior is learned, and it's good for teens to learn that getting your work done leads to a financial reward. When the TV show *Friends* first came on the air, most of the people in the group were gleefully underemployed, yet somehow they enjoyed lavish lifestyles. A lot of young people grow up expecting that, when they reach adulthood, that's what their lives are going to be like—and it's not. Parents do kids a disservice if they spoon-feed children so much that when the children move out on their own, they don't know how to live within their means.

Teens have the ability to earn money beyond their allowances. One way is to do things for you that you would have to pay somebody else to do. Another is by working for others. Younger teens can do odd jobs such as yard work or washing cars. Older teens can work outside the home. So the allowance you give them is just a base.

When teens do things above and beyond their regular responsibilities, you should pay them. Such "bonus chores" include mowing the lawn, washing the car, and babysitting younger children. Some parents don't think they should pay a teen to babysit his siblings. But I think paying your teen something—half the going rate—will make your teen more responsible. If the going rate is $8 to $10 an hour, pay your son $4 to $5. If he's smart, he'll want to earn the market rate working for another family, and I'm fine with that, because it gets him into the entrepreneurial spirit.

Teens' allowances should pay for movie tickets, music, and the like, as well as set up choices. Ten dollars a week might not be enough for a tenth-grader to see a movie both Friday and Saturday nights, unless there are bargain shows—such as matinees or early evening—or second-run theaters. Or they could see one movie at night at the full retail price, or do some extra chores that week to earn extra money.

Until I came up with my $1 per grade system, I struggled with allowance. For a while we tried giving my older daughter a pretty significant allowance—$20 a week. Rebecca's mother, Karen, and I came up with that amount, and the plan was that Rebecca would use that to buy the things she wanted, so that she wouldn't constantly plead with us for money. But we were never able to execute that successfully. Rebecca used her allowance to buy CDs and clothing, but there were still things she would convince one of us to pay for that were supposed to come out of the allowance. Rebecca spends time at her mother's house and at mine, so even though Karen and I have the best of intentions and we communicate very well, it was hard to enforce a consistent policy.

Now we exclude clothes from her allowance. We buy clothes for her, and she uses her allowance for music, movies, and teen stuff.

Rebecca, who is fifteen, works as a babysitter, and she has chores around the house. Rebecca has to make her bed every day, just as Lane and I do each day. Rebecca also has to put her dirty clothes in the hamper and she has to put her makeup away. That one I'm losing on. The bathroom looks like a cosmetics counter, with everything scattered about. What does this have to do with money? Creating a sense of personal responsibility in how you do things in your life is part of the picture in what happens with money.

Jonathan Clements, the personal finance columnist for the *Wall Street Journal*, says that you have to give children a sense of ownership, so they view allowance as their money, rather than money that you give them. Clements recommends this experiment: The next time you go to the mall, give your child $10 to spend, and tell her you want change back. You won't get much back. Try it again a week later, but this time tell your child that she can keep the change. Your child won't spend as much money, because she looks at the money as hers rather than yours.

I've seen this with adults at work. When we're on company travel, people spend money far more freely than they would their own money. And they joke about it. It drives me crazy how carelessly people spend other people's money. When I was in the travel business, I used to encourage companies to reward employees who spent less than they were allowed by splitting the savings with them. If they stayed at a friend's house instead of a hotel, I encouraged them to give the employee half of what the company would have spent if the employee had stayed at a hotel. Travel expenses collapse when you do that, because there's a huge incentive for people to save.

Human nature works with children as well. You just have to come up with ways for your kids to see the benefit, short-term or long-term. One thing that's a given about allowance is there's no incentive not to spend it. If you teach your child to spend all of his allowance each week, he might learn to spend all of his paycheck as an adult. Instead, tell him that you'll double whatever allowance he has left after a significant period of time, every six months or at the end of the year. That's a hefty incentive to save, and even a child who's in grade school can think ahead to the end of the year.

You can get teens interested in saving by opening a savings account with them. Earning interest is always a good incentive to save.

If your teen has a Palm, Pocket PC, or PDA, have him track where his allowance goes using the money software that's usu- ally included with these devices or can be downloaded for free. Your teen can create charts showing how he's spending his money. I've spoken and written about adults using a notepad to write down when they spend money, so they can see where their money goes. This is a more so- phisticated way of doing the same thing, for a generation that's very comfortable with PDAs and "smart" cell phones. Kids love technology.

✳ The Clark Smart Allowance Plan for Teens ✳

• How Much to Pay •

Ninth grade:	$9 a week
Tenth grade:	$10 a week
Eleventh grade:	$11 a week
Twelfth grade:	$12 a week

• Basic Chores •

Make the bed
Clean room

• Rotating Family Chores (the Chore Wheel) •

Feed pets
Take out the garbage
Put away groceries
Laundry

• Bonus Chores •

Grocery shopping	$5
Babysit for younger kids	$4–$5 an hour
Mow the lawn	$8 an hour
Landscaping/planting flowers	$8 an hour
Rake leaves	$8 an hour
Shovel snow from driveway	$8 an hour
Clean the pool	$8 an hour
Clean the bathroom	$8 an hour
Cook dinner	$5
Wash parents' car	$3
Detail the car	$10

✳ Where Does Your Family Fit In? ✳

My daughter Rebecca, at fifteen, astonished me by asking, "Are we comfortable financially?"

We live a very comfortable life and, by national standards, we're wealthy. But Rebecca doesn't know yet where she fits on the financial spectrum. She has no concept because she goes to private school and she's around families that either are wealthy or pretend to be, with the flash they have in their lives. We volunteer at a homeless shelter at least once a year, so she can appreciate the need to help others who aren't as fortunate as she is. But what I realized is that she sees poor people as one category financially, then has no concept of where everybody else is on the continuum.

A friend told me about another teenager whose parents were worth $25 to $50 million. The girl asked her father, "Daddy, do we know any millionaires?" She had no idea that her parents were millionaires. Another child, the son of the CEO of a Fortune 500 company, lives in a modest house on Long Island, New York. He came home one day and handed his dad a financial aid application for college. The father told him to just worry about getting admitted to the school and that they wouldn't be needing any financial aid.

If you are in the top 25 percent of income earners (with an adjusted gross income of $56,000 or more, according to the last U.S. Census), you have to get across to your child that he isn't going to be able to immediately duplicate the lifestyle he enjoyed as he was growing up. That's the core of affluenza. If your kids don't have a feel for that, they're going to have problems when they finish school and don't understand why they can't have a luxury car or a new home or a fancy apartment on the entry-level salary they earn on their first jobs.

Most teenagers have a startlingly inaccurate view of how much their parents earn or what it costs to buy things. My coauthor had a chat with his grandchildren about money, and he was fascinated by how they perceived money at their preteen ages. Courtney, who was ten at the time, thought $2,000 would be a good annual salary for someone to earn, and her brother Nicholas, who was twelve, thought $9,000 would be a good salary. So Mark asked how much they thought things cost. Courtney thought a new Volkswagen Beetle would cost $1,000. Both kids thought it cost about $100 a month to rent a house. Even

though they were well beyond their toddler years—Nicholas was in the seventh grade at the time—they had almost no idea how the financial world works. That they didn't know what things cost at ten and twelve years old means there probably is no discussion in their home about it.

Want to know what your teen would say? Make a list of the things you spend money on each month. If you have a formal budget, get that out. Then give your kid a second list with the budget categories and have him fill in the numbers and estimate your income as well. I'll bet the answers will surprise you.

You can help your kids learn about the cost of things by talking more about this. At the age it's appropriate, and that's different in each family, have a series of discussions about what houses cost, what apartments cost, and what cars cost.

Tell your teenager what your mortgage payment or rent is each month. Tell him how much of a down payment you made when you bought the house, what the house cost, and what it's worth now. If you have a car loan, tell him what that payment is per month, and how much you pay for gas, oil changes, and insurance. Tell your teen that when you finish paying off your car loan, you can keep driving the car without having to make that payment every month. He'll have a million questions for you, because this is about his life. Teach him that money is a finite resource and that you have to set priorities. I like to think of money as a snowball. You can push it uphill, and at some point it might get too big and fall back and crush you. Or you can roll it downhill, and it will get bigger and bigger, creating more security and comfort for you.

You can talk to your children about everything you spend money on—from clothes to teeth cleanings. Pull out your check register or online statement to show them. If you give regularly to charity, tell your children about that. If you feel comfortable opening up, you can create a bond with your child that will last forever and give you a chance to teach them. This is not one discussion. It's many discussions.

If you have a very organized, responsible teen, consider having her help you pay the household bills online. Make it part of her basic chores, or a bonus chore to earn extra allowance. She'll learn about the household budget and help you at the same time.

You can use houses in your neighborhood to help your child understand the costs of owning a home. Find a house that's for sale. Even if you have no interest in buying the house, pick up the flyer for it, which will describe the house and list a selling price. You can talk to your child about how much a house costs, what the monthly payment would be, what the property taxes would cost. Then you have to add in utilities. You could compare it to your house, or let your child make the comparison. You could figure out how much you'd have to earn to afford the house. Real estate magazines, often available in supermarkets, are a good tool for teaching your son or daughter what houses cost.

Realtor.com is another good source for housing information. You can show your child what an average house costs in your area, and what it looks like, and what a mansion costs. Because kids are in houses every day, they're one of the easiest ways to explain your relative financial position.

You can take it a step further by figuring out what the mortgage payment might be on a house your child is interested in. Go to www.bankrate.com or www. monstermoving.com or www.hsh.com, find out what current mortgage rates are, and use the mortgage calculators to determine the monthly principal and interest payment on a mortgage. For example, if the house costs $150,000 and you put 10 percent down ($15,000), that means you're borrowing $135,000. At an interest rate of 6.5 percent, the payments on a thirty-year mortgage would be a little more than $900. Taxes and insurance are extra. You can easily print out an amortization schedule that shows what you would pay per month for the life of the loan (for 30 years, that's 360 monthly payments). The schedule shows you how much of each payment is applied to interest, and how little of it in the early years actually goes to pay down the purchase price of the house. Look five years down the road, at payment number sixty, and you'll see that in this example you've reduced the principal only $8,000.

You can explain the down payment this way: Lenders take on risk when they loan you the money to buy a house, so they want a down payment to reduce their risk that you won't pay back the loan. The more you put down, the less risk there is for the lender. If you put down less than 20 percent, you'll also have to pay for private mortgage insurance, which further protects the lender.

My mother-in-law used to be a real estate agent, so as a child, the cost of houses was the one financial thing Lane really understood. She'd go to open houses with her mom and hear all this talk about monthly payments, so she was immersed in it without even realizing it. That's what I want you to do with your children. Regardless of age, and using different techniques at different ages, help your kids learn about what people earn and how much things cost.

• Internet •

www.bankrate.com	*(Mortgage rates and calculators)*
www.hsh.com	*(Mortgage rates and calculators)*
www.monstermoving.com	*(Mortgage rates and calculators)*
www.realtor.com	*(House prices)*

⁕ Ten Questions to Ask Your Teen ⁕

What kind of car do you want to drive when you're an adult?

How much do you think that would cost?

What do you think it would cost per month? (Loan payment, gas, insurance, maintenance, and depreciation—the loss in the car's value as it ages)

How much would it cost to rent an apartment?

When you live on your own, how much do you think a week's groceries would cost?

How much would you expect to pay each month for utilities? (Gas or heating oil, electricity, water, phone)

Do you know what "take-home pay" is?

How much do you think four years of college costs?

How much does it cost for a family of four to eat dinner at a mid-priced restaurant, such as the Outback Steakhouse, Chili's, or Romano's Macaroni Grill?

How much would a family vacation to Disney World cost?

⁕ Teens and Cars ⁕

Instead of buying your teenager a new car, I believe you should either buy him a clunker or make him buy his own clunker. Then, make him pay for the insurance, gas, oil changes, and other maintenance. You want your teenager to have a sense of ownership in the vehicle. If you don't create a sense of ownership, your child won't take care of the car. It's like someone who rents an apartment versus someone who owns a home. Teenagers need that pride of ownership, as well as the responsibility of coming up with the money every month for an insurance premium, repairs, and gas. It makes a big difference in their willingness to take care of the car. Just don't let them work more hours than you are comfortable with to pay for the car.

Joni Alpert, who works on my radio

show, had her twin daughters pool their money from child-care and pet-sitting jobs to come up with $3,000 to buy a car. Joni and her husband, Hal, matched the $3,000, and added another $500 to get to the $6,500 they spent on the girls' first car. It may not have been as much fun as getting a shiny new car, but the girls were thrilled nonetheless.

Rebecca's mother, Karen, is buying her a clunker. Karen bought an old Saturn for $2,500, and is going to drive it herself until Rebecca is sixteen. One of the reasons to give a teenager a clunker— and a cell phone in case it breaks down— is so you don't have to buy collision or comprehensive insurance. You or your teenager will have to buy only liability insurance, which is to protect you and your teenager if he causes damage in an accident. Collision coverage is expensive, and you don't need it with a very inexpensive car. If the car is wrecked, you junk it and start over.

Certain vehicles are safer for teenagers to drive. The best choice is a dull, used, mid-sized sedan, such as the Honda Accord, Toyota Camry, or Ford Taurus, all with four-cylinder engines. You want your teenager's car to go from zero to sixty miles per hour in two days. No horses under the hood. That's exactly the opposite of what most teenagers want to drive, but safer.

When you make a teenager responsible for insurance and upkeep, you're saying she's going to have to work part-time to support her automobile. Most states have a minimum driving age of sixteen or seventeen, which is an age when it's fine to work fifteen hours a week. So at $6 an hour, your teen could work fifteen hours a week and make $90 a week, or $360 a month. That's plenty for her to afford insurance and maintenance.

If your teenager gets a ticket, he should pay for it. It's the logical consequence of his action. When teens or adults get tickets in most states, they can wipe out the points that go on their licenses by taking a driver safety class. What a great motivation for them to take the class. It will keep their insurance rates from soaring and they'll learn important defensive driving techniques as well.

Another thing I recommend is take your teen to traffic court. It's quite an eye-opener to see what happens when you don't obey the law.

✳ Filling Up ✳

If your teen is driving for the first time, please explain to her that she should buy discount gasoline. You have an opportunity to set a lifelong habit. Fewer than a third of adults actually shop for gas strictly on price, and that's a shame. Because gas is gas, no matter where you buy it. Why not teach your teen early on that gas can be purchased at an off-brand gas station or a discount store for savings of 15 to 20 cents a gallon. That's $1.50 to $2 in savings every fill-up for a ten-gallon tank, more for bigger vehicles. Again, little choices you make add up over time into big money. It's very important for teens, especially for girls, to never let the tank go below a third full. It's dangerous for teens to drive on fumes and risk running out of gas.

✳ The Cost of Insurance ✳

There are a variety of factors that will af-fect how much you, or your child, pay for auto insurance, including whether you buy full coverage (including collision coverage) or just liability coverage, whether your child has good grades and has taken a driver's training course (either in school or from a private company), what kind of vehicle you buy, whether your child is the car's primary driver, and whether you have a son or daughter. Girls cost less to insure than boys. Children with good grades and driver training are eligible for discounts.

Rates also vary widely depending on where you live and which insurer you choose. It's very important to shop with multiple insurance companies, because every insurer looks at risk differently, so you will get dramatically different quotes from different companies. The difference for a young driver could be as much as $1,000 a year.

But here's a look from a State Farm agent near my home in Atlanta at how different factors can affect rates. A seventeen-year-old boy who is the primary driver of his car and who carries only liability coverage would pay about $694 every six months, or about $116 a month. The rate drops to $526 every six months if he has and maintains a 3.0 grade-point average at school. Add a driver's training class and it drops to $471 every six months. Good grades are worth more than driver training. If the boy has driver training but no discount for good grades, he'd pay $622 every six months.

If this boy is listed as an occasional driver, the rate is lower. State Farm allows you to do that if a family has, say, two adults and two cars, and the teenager is listed as an occasional driver on one car. If the family has two adults and three cars, the teenager has to be a primary driver. The seventeen-year-old would pay just $432 every six months as an occasional driver, versus $694 as a primary driver. With a good-student discount, the rate drops to $329 every six months. Add driver's training, and the rate drops to $296.

If the driver is a seventeen-year-old girl, she would pay $375 every six months if she's the primary driver, $303 if she is an occasional driver. If she has good grades and driver's training, she could pay as little as $307 every six months as the primary driver, $249 if she is listed as an occasional driver.

It's far more expensive if you buy collision coverage, and you also have to consider what kind of car you're buying, because seemingly similar cars might cost more or less to insure. For example, a seventeen-year-old boy with a basic full-coverage insurance policy (primary driver) on a 2002 Mazda Millenia would pay $2,438 every six months, or $406 a month (without any discounts). If that same boy bought a 2002 Honda Accord LX instead, the cost would drop to $1,890 every six months, or $315 a month. So it's vital to check the cost to insure the car you want to buy before you buy it.

The discounts mean even more for full coverage, because they're a percentage of the total cost. So the seventeen-year-old boy would cut his cost to insure the Accord to $1,424 every six months ($237 a month) with good grades and $1,271 ($212 a month) with both good grades and driver's training. If he were an occasional driver, the cost would be $1,164 ($194 a month) with no discounts, $877 ($146 a month) with good grades, and $788 ($131 a month) with good grades and driver's training.

Driver's education is a good thing, and I think it's great for you and your teenager to split the cost of it. There's an insurance savings for it, and they will be more invested in the class if they're paying a portion of the cost. But it's not enough. The most important education is the one your teenager gets watching you drive, because the example you set behind the wheel sets her pattern. If you run red lights, turn without signaling, and aggressively tailgate other cars, your child will do the same. Kids learn by example, so if you drive poorly and your child is approaching driving age, that's a wake-up call for you to drive more safely.

Even if your child takes driver's education, you still need to spend a lot of time with her behind the wheel. I started teaching Rebecca to drive when she was thirteen. We go to office parks on the weekends, when no one's there, and practice in the parking lot. I teach her, and she practices how to back up, how to turn right, how to turn left, and how to approach an intersection. Statistics show hands down that the more experience you have behind the wheel, the better a driver you are going to be. Driver's education is only a small part of the equation.

I also would like to see you sign a contract with your teen that will govern her driving behavior; you can download one from Dale Wisely's Web site, www. parentingteendrivers.com

✳ How to Buy a Car ✳

Your teenager's first car is probably the most expensive thing he will buy before adulthood, and it's a great opportunity to teach him the right way to buy a car. When you talk about money in theory, a kid can zone out. But if he knows this will translate into his wheels, you'll have his full attention. Take him with you through each step of the process, and let him do some of the legwork. You set the price range, and tell him which models will be acceptable. Have him research the cars online, using Consumer Reports (www.consumerreports.org, a subscription service) for quality and Edmunds (www.edmunds.com) and Kelley Blue Book (www.kbb.com) for price. The price you pay for a used car should be somewhere between the average trade-in price and the average retail price. The average trade-in, what the dealer probably paid the previous owner, is the lower price. Bring your child with you when you negotiate the price of the car. Just make sure he doesn't tell the dealer he loves the car, because it's harder to negotiate if the dealer knows you'll buy no matter what the price.

You can also have your teenager check the cost to insure each of the models you're considering, since he will be paying for the insurance. And when you select a car you may buy, let your child test-drive the car, and take him with you when you get the car inspected for quality by a diagnostic mechanic. This is a step you can't skip, and it can be a real eye-opener for your child. Look for someone with an ASE certification, an indication that the mechanic has the expertise needed to do a comprehensive evaluation. It's well worth the $100 or so you'll spend to make sure the vehicle has no major defects and hasn't been in an accident. A wreck can cause a car to have tremendous operating problems as well as suffer a huge loss in value. The only way to know whether it's been in an accident is to have it inspected.

The diagnostic tests aren't pass or fail. Sometimes, the mechanic will report that a part is worn, and you'll have to make the decision whether to buy the car. You can also use the disclosure of certain problems as leverage to lower the price. Then you can use the savings to pay for repairs.

My coauthor helped his stepson Keith buy a used van and was able to save Keith more than $1,000. The dealer wanted $6,000 for the van, which wasn't a bad price, and Keith was willing to pay it. But Mark negotiated the price down to below $5,000. The diagnostic inspection showed the vehicle was sound but needed a few hundred dollars' worth of work. Mark and Keith showed the dealer the diagnostic report, and he agreed to deduct the cost of the work needed from the purchase price. They talked about the trade-in price, which was a good deal below the $6,000 retail price the dealer was asking. That helped move the price down further. Finally, Mark and Keith offered to write a check on the spot if the dealer would sell the van for their price, which was $4,700. He agreed.

If you buy a used car at a dealership that doesn't offer you the opportunity to return the car for a refund, make your deal for the purchase contingent on its passing an inspection by a diagnostic mechanic. Then have it inspected before you complete the purchase. If a seller refuses to allow the vehicle to be inspected, don't buy it.

In addition to having a used car inspected, it's a very good idea to pay about $20 to pull a report on the car at www.carfax.com (you need the vehicle identification number, or VIN, to do this). Carfax will run a history of the car's title instantly, plus do a free check to see if the car has been part of a Lemon Law buyback. The title history can help you determine if the car's odometer has been rolled back or disconnected.

Most used-car sales in the United States still are as-is sales, with no warranty to protect you. If you buy from an individual, don't expect a warranty. But if you pay more to buy from a dealer, you have a right to expect some protection if the car doesn't work once you've purchased it.

The law is of minimal help. Only a handful of states provide any legal protection for used-car buyers. In many other states, you own the car as soon as you sign the papers.

Some unethical dealers still sell worthless cars salvaged from wrecks. The paperwork is washed, and you could buy a vehicle that actually is two or three cars sewn together. To minimize the danger of buying a problem-ridden car, do not buy from old-style dealers who sell only used cars. When a new-car dealer takes a trade or a return from a rental company, it keeps the best vehicles on its lot and sells the rest through auction. The most troubled cars end up at used-car lots. The worst used-car lots are the "Buy Here, Pay Here" lots. Almost always, the cars are incidental to the purpose of these places. They make their money on the car loans they extend to customers. They're in the loan business, not the car business.

You can find available used cars at a number of Web sites, including www.autotrader.com and www.carmax.com. Have your child look for, say, Ford Tauruses for less than $5,000. Help him come up with a list of questions to ask and then have him call the dealer.

If you don't like negotiating the cost of a car and don't want to get ripped off on the price, a good place to turn to is CarMax. If you're not familiar with CarMax, it's a company that's expanding rapidly around the country. By the time you read this, CarMax will be new in a lot of cities. CarMax sells used cars with no-haggle pricing. The price on the window is the price you pay. It's a great no-pressure environment to buy a used car. CarMax's price probably won't be the lowest in the market, but it'll be a reasonable price, and they give you five days to return the car if you don't like it. That's plenty of time to have the car checked by a mechanic. It's a good place to go search for a moderately priced used car. There's a large selection, which you can search online at www.carmax.com. Even if you don't buy from CarMax, you can use CarMax's prices as leverage if you buy elsewhere.

If you choose to buy an ultra-inexpensive car ($5,000 or below), you're probably going to have to buy it from a private seller, rather than a car dealer. Used-car dealers want the same markup for a used car no matter what the price range. You'll have to work harder, really go out and look, and you'll hit a lot of dead ends. But it is possible to buy a decent car for less than $5,000. *Consumer Reports* puts out lists of reliable, inexpensive used cars, but the magazine doesn't list cars that cost less than $6,000. The list appears in the magazine's annual April auto issue, which you can find at the library or online. In the ultra-inexpensive category, there's one car that's my favorite. Its name has changed through model years, but you'll see it as either the Chevy Prism or Geo Prism. It's the ultimate used-car special because it's actually a Toyota Corolla, but under a marketing arrangement between the companies, it's sold under the Chevy or Geo name. So you get Toyota reliability at a big discount. It's a little small, which is a safety issue, but it's a great choice as a value car.

A lot of parents will give their sport utility vehicle to their teenager after mom or dad gets tired of driving it. But you should never put a teenager behind the wheel of a sport utility vehicle or a Jeep. It's tremendously dangerous, to the teen and to others. These vehicles have very high centers of gravity and are more prone to rollover accidents than regular cars. They're too hard to handle for a young, inexperienced driver. Think of these vehicles the way you think of a poison bottle with a skull and crossbones on it. Don't do it.

I was driving Rebecca to school and we saw one of Rebecca's older schoolmates driving to school. He went through a stop sign like he didn't see it, and he was driving a high-horsepower, two-door sports car. Fortunately, there was no accident, but what in the world were his parents thinking? Her high school is small enough that she knows the older students, so she said, "Yeah, that's so-and-so." And I said, "You're not riding with him."

There's plenty of debate over how old your children should be before they get their driver's licenses. Now that I'm the parent of a fifteen-year-old, I think the driving age should be about thirty-five. I intend to let my children get their driver's licenses at seventeen, because the leap in maturity from sixteen to seventeen makes a big difference. I got my own driver's license when I was sixteen, and I was so excited I actually had a countdown calendar marking off the days to my sixteenth birthday. Then at the test location, we got turned away because my mother had an expired inspection sticker on her car. She borrowed a neighbor's Electra 225, the longest car ever made, for my test. You should have seen me parallel parking that car. That officer was sure he was going to be able to flunk me, but I passed. He took sixteen points off for inattention. He said anybody who talks as much as I do could not possibly be paying attention to his driving.

For more on how to buy a new or used car, please see my previous book, *Get Clark Smart*.

• Internet •

www.autotrader.com	*(Available used cars)*
www.carfax.com	*(Vehicle history report)*
www.carmax.com	*(Available used cars, price comparisons)*
www.consumerreports.org	*(Car quality ratings)*
www.edmunds.com	*(Used car prices)*
www.kbb.com	*(Used car prices)*
www.parentingteendrivers.com	*(Driving contract for teens)*

✳Understanding Credit Cards and Cash Machines✳

You can teach a child that money is lim-ited by using cash instead of credit and debit cards, but as they grow up you're going to have to teach them about plastic.

Most people know I hate debit cards, because errors can foul up your checking account, and they don't offer the same protections as real credit cards. But in spite of all that, I think debit cards are a great teaching tool for teenagers. Your teen has to keep track of her balance with her "fake Visa" card, so she doesn't over-draft her account. Many banks will allow a teenager to have a free checking account, because they hope they will stay loyal to that bank as they grow older. I recom-mend you try this at the age you think is appropriate for your child, perhaps as young as thirteen. Some banks require the child to be fifteen, but others will allow a child to open a checking account at what-ever age the parent wants to do it. You open the account and put money into it, and then the teen uses a check register to track the balance. Each time your son uses the card, he notes the amount he spent and deducts it from the balance. If he has $130 in his account and he wants to buy

an iPod for $199, he doesn't have enough. This teaches him that plastic is not an infi-nite source of money.

I've heard from listeners that adults are doing this as well, even with real credit cards. They use an old-fashioned, hand-written check register for their checking ac-count, and each time they use their credit cards, they deduct the amount they spend from their checking account balance. Psy-chologically, it helps them see that if they charge too much, they're going to be broke. Under this system, if you have $500 in your checking account and you charge something for $100, you reduce your checking account balance to $400. It makes it impossible to reconcile your checking account balance, but it gives you more financial discipline because the mes-sage is "I spent the money." Eventually, you will write a check from your checking account to cover what you charged. And if you don't, you'll start running a balance, paying interest and getting into credit card trouble. My listeners have taught me that using a check register with your credit card can turn what seems like an unlimited supply of money into a limited supply.

Why not just write a check when you buy something? The number of checks being written has declined dramatically, in part because many retailers, especially in the South and West, no longer accept checks.

Some 20 percent of Americans—maybe 40 million adults—don't carry a credit card anymore, some because they can't get one, others because they know they can't use credit without getting into trouble. Some use debit cards, which offer some of the convenience of credit cards without the chance that you could spend more than you have.

You can teach financial discipline to a child by giving her a debit card when you think she's ready for one. That will lay the groundwork for getting a credit card in college. Make sure, however, that your teen doesn't use a debit card to buy gasoline. Gas stations often put a hold on hundreds of dollars in your checking account when you use a debit card (hotels do the same thing, with even more money), and that hold makes a lot of your money unavailable to you for perhaps a week.

Using a check register with a credit or debit card makes you accountable for each purchase, just as you would be if you used cash. If you can teach children to do this when they're thirteen or fourteen, that habit may well stick with them the rest of their lives. And you know what? Lead by example. If you know you're not as disciplined as you'd like to be in using credit, use a check register to track your own credit card purchases. If they see you do it, it'll help reinforce the message.

Before your child is thirteen, you can help her understand credit cards and debit cards by talking about them. Kids may act as though they're tuning you out, but they learn anyway. Listen to what your child says to you. If she says, "Why don't you just charge it," that's your cue to give them the message, early and often, that there's only so much the credit card can stand (your credit line) and that you have to use the money you make at work to pay for the purchases anyway. Plus, if you put too much on it, you won't have enough to pay it off at the end of the month, and you'll get hit with big charges called interest. If you spend $20 on it and take too long to pay it back, you might have to pay $25, and you don't want to do that. Your child will understand.

In my book *Clark's Big Book of Bar-*

gains, I wrote about software designer David Hunt, who created a program called Family Bank (www.parentware.org) that helps teach children six to sixteen about money and about borrowing. Parents deposit a child's weekly allowance in an account, from which the child can withdraw it to spend or save it. If they want more money, they can borrow it, but they have to pay it back with interest. So instead of getting $10 a week, they might receive $8.50 a week until the loan is repaid. It's an early lesson in the dangers of credit card abuse.

When your child is a teen, show him your credit card statement. Show him what you spent that month, and how much interest you paid. Even if you didn't pay interest, show him the box that describes how much you would pay if you didn't pay in full. The percentage of people who pay in full each month has fallen, and now only a little more than a third do so. Some two-thirds do not pay in full each month and are forced to pay high interest charges. If you're hurting from having to pay interest, use your experience as a way to help your child. Tell them you're coming up with a plan to pay your credit card debt so you don't have to pay interest anymore.

✳ Teens and Credit ✳

As soon as your son or daughter arrives at college, he or she will see people handing out free T-shirts, Frisbees, towels, and a number of other items. All the new collegian will have to do to get one of the freebies is sign up for a credit card. It's the craziest thing. The student doesn't have to demonstrate any source of income, employment history, credit history—nothing. If you're a freshman enrolling full-time at a college, you are going to have more credit thrown your way than you could have imagined existed. All the credit card companies are there to get in your wallet or purse.

Credit card companies love college students because they are the most profitable customers that they have ever seen or ever will see. That's because college students don't pay their balance in full at the end of every month, and college credit cards carry very high interest rates, usually around 20 percent. Yet the risk to the lender is very low, because when trouble comes, Mommy and Daddy step in. College kids typically get a credit card with a $1,000 limit, and to them that means "I can buy $1,000 worth of pizza." Then the bill comes in, and they don't even consider paying it in full. The monthly minimum is the amount they see as the payment due. So the interest meter keeps running and running.

Some students get so many credit cards that they can't make the payments, then the mean bill collector calls and screams at them, so the student calls Mommy or Daddy, who then pays the bills.

I don't have a problem with college students having credit cards, because having a credit card, and using it wisely, can help a young person establish a credit record. That will help when it comes time to buy a car, and later, a house. And many teens just want to be independent. They aren't looking to blow all of their (or your) money.

When I was in college, before they started handing out cards like candy, I was also working full-time, and I got a credit card. I never got into trouble with it, because somehow even then I knew to pay the balance in full. I was able to get a car loan on my own because I had a good credit record. Taking advantage of the opportunity to get one credit card, or at most two, when a student is a freshman, is a great thing. But as a parent you should teach your child, starting around the tenth grade, what to do when he gets to college and gets credit for the first time. Part of the appeal of a credit card to a student is that he doesn't need Mom or Dad to get one. It's like a rite of passage, being able to get money directly from the bank without his parents. Students think the bank is their buddy, and they don't realize how crippling the interest payments can be. If a teen buys a $40 lamp for his dorm room from Target, and pays the minimum 2 percent on the balance each month with an 18 percent interest rate, it would take ninety-one months and $72.16 to pay it off.

Tell your kids to get one or two credit cards, but no more, and talk to them about what can happen if they abuse credit. There are some nightmare stories of kids who ended up with eight or ten credit cards by the time they were juniors, and every one of the cards was maxed out. The kids get addicted to the lifestyle. If a kid wants a new stereo, he puts it on a credit card. One girl I spoke with racked up $15,000 in debt and had to drop out of school to pay the bills.

Even some high school students now have credit cards—one in ten high school students now carries a Visa or MasterCard.

Sometimes high school kids get credit cards by having a parent co-sign, or college students get car loans by having parents co-sign. But parents should be very, very careful about co-signing things for their children. If you co-sign a loan to help your son or daughter get a car, you put your credit and your money at risk. If your child doesn't pay, you have to pay. But the risk is limited to the cost of the car, plus interest. If you co-sign for a credit-card, the risk is open-ended, so I strongly recommend you don't co-sign for a credit card. Even with the car loan, I'd prefer that, rather than co-sign, you act as the bank yourself. Pay for the car and have your child pay you back. When you co-sign a car loan, you could theoretically step in and make the payments if your child stopped making them. That way, you could protect your own credit rating. But you might not know if your child made the car payment or not. About every other week I get a call from someone who has co-signed a car loan for a relative, and he has no idea of the risk involved in lending his credit to someone. These people give no thought to the consequences if their boyfriend, girlfriend, brother, sister, son, daughter, or whoever doesn't pay for the car. The worst situation is if the car gets repossessed. Then you get no benefit from the car, but you're stuck with the amount still owed and your credit gets ruined for seven years.

There are alternatives to a credit card if you'd like your child to have the convenience of credit without all of the risk. One is the debit card, which is linked to a checking account (see Understanding Credit Cards and Cash Machines). Another is the stored-value card. You get a card with a Visa, MasterCard, or American Express logo on it that can be used anywhere those cards are accepted, and put an amount of money on the card, say $300 or $500, which becomes the limit of the card. It eliminates the problem of running up a balance. The first generation of these cards has been too expensive, but I hope that will change. American Express's card, for example, charges you $5 every time you want to add money to the card. Some have fees every time you use the card and/or monthly fees. But prepaid phone cards were a ripoff when they started, and over time they became one of the cheapest ways to make long-distance calls. I think the same thing will happen with stored-value cards. There are gift cards that are similar, but they don't have the user's name on them.

✳ Should Your Child Get a Student Loan? ✳

Two-thirds of undergraduate students have at least some student-loan debt when they graduate, according to Finaid.org. The average student-loan debt for an undergraduate now is $18,900, but it jumps to $45,900 for graduate students and $91,700 for law and medical students.

Student loans may carry very favorable rates of interest and can be paid off over a period of time equivalent to a home mortgage, but they also require a very serious, long-term commitment on the part of the borrower. If you take out a student loan for your child, you will be responsible for paying it back. If your child takes the loan out, it is his or her burden to bear. If student loans seem like your student's best option, I recommend you let him take the loan out. I have two reasons for suggesting this. One is practical—your student is likely to have a lower income than you will in the first five years after graduation, when the loan interest is tax deductible up to a certain income threshold. Second, I want your student to have the very grown-up responsibility of having to repay the loan after school.

Student loans can damage your child's credit if he doesn't pay them on time. The consequences of defaulting on a student loan are severe. Your child's credit rating will plunge, which could make it difficult for them to buy a car, rent an apartment, or even get a job. Payments could be deducted from his paycheck. Income tax refunds could be withheld to pay for the defaulted loan, students have to pay collection fees on top of what they already owe, and they can be sued. Those are pretty stiff penalties for failing to pay, so taking out a loan should be done with a great deal of forethought.

For a comprehensive guide to student loans, check out the government's Web site at www.ed.gov.

Alternatives to Student Loans

I recommend you and your teen avoid the burden of heavy student loan debt and look for creative methods to pay for school. I'm a big advocate of students taking additional time to graduate, and working full-time or part-time while they take classes. So many of the expenses of school are living expenses. If a job can cover the cost of housing and food while you're in school, you're ahead of the game when you graduate.

If your student wants to go into a profession that is in demand right now, she may qualify for a student loan forgiveness program. For example, there is a federal teaching program that will pay for a portion of a child's student loans if she teaches in a needy school for five or more years after graduating. Many states also have their own loan forgiveness programs and will even assist teachers with down payments on houses in exchange for an agreement to remain in a school for a period of time. Nursing is another profession that is in critical need of new recruits. There are many programs similar to the teaching student-loan forgiveness programs run by hospitals that will help a student pay for school if they agree to work for the hospital.

Another alternative is to take advantage of the education benefits many employers provide. You could go to work full-time for an employer that offers this benefit, and attend school at night. I went to graduate school for free because I was working at IBM, and they paid all tuition if your degree was related to your employment. I worked, believe it or not, as a bill collector, collecting money from the federal government, and I got a master's degree in management. So I had free tuition, plus a full-time salary, at age twenty-one, and I finished graduate school owing no money at all. I worked for the government as an undergraduate, which paid a lot of the cost of getting my bachelor's degree.

There are also an untold number of scholarships available to college students. Don't pay any of the companies that want to charge you a fee to have access to information about scholarships—the information is free on the Internet and from the schools themselves.

If your child is already set on one particular school, have him talk to the financial aid department about student scholarships set up for the school. Many alumni offer scholarships to students who meet certain criteria, which can be anything from ethnicity or gender to the student's major. If your child attends a private high school, there are often scholarships set up by alumni for graduates of the school. Have your child ask his guidance counselor about what is available. Local communities and clubs also may have scholarships that counselors at school may be aware of.

There are some great places on the Web to search for scholarships as well. Some I really like are www.scholar ships.com, www.fastweb.com, and www .studentaid.org.

If you think your family might qualify for financial aid, make sure you visit the Web site of the free application for federal student aid at www.fafsa.ed.gov.

I've had many parents ask me if they should have their teen contribute some of her earnings from a job to a college savings fund. While the thought is great, I'd much rather see your child open a Roth IRA with that money, because the tax-free growth over her working lifetime on that money will be worth much more than saving the money for college.

It's also more important to create the early habit of saving for the long-term than saving for college. There are so many ways to pay for college, that I don't see saving for college as a priority.

One way your teen can help contribute to the cost of college is to become an RA, or resident adviser. That's a dormitory position in which the student supervises other students, making sure the college's rules on alcohol, parties, and the like are followed. RAs also arrange social events. It teaches responsibility and leadership, as well as reducing the cost of college. Christa DiBiase, executive producer of my radio show, was an RA in college and got a free private room for her last two years in college, plus a food card that was good for free meals as well as toiletries.

Her father was very happy with that, and strongly encouraged her to remain an RA her final year, rather than get an off-campus apartment with friends.

A Special Note About Law and Medical School

There are many alternative programs for both lawyers and doctors that may help ease the financial burdens they face with huge student loans. There are opportunities for lawyers to extend their schooling into a four-year program instead of the traditional three years it usually takes to earn a J.D. You attend school year-round at night, and you work full-time, which lowers your cost a great deal. If you can get a job in a law firm, so much the better. You end up going to school for forty-eight straight months instead of the eight months a year you would go in a three-year program. Shortening school for med students is also a great alternative. There are many colleges that have both pre-med and medical schools that will allow the student to combine undergraduate and graduate school in a five-year M.D. program. One example of such a school is Rutgers, a state university in New Jersey. Students can obtain both their Bachelor of Arts and their M.D. in seven years, trimming at least a year of tuition from their student loan bills.

✳ What's in a Name? ✳

The cachet of attending a top private college is not what it used to be. You have to decide whether going to a big-name school is worth the enormous cost. If going to one school forces you to take out $50,000 in student loans, while going to another school would allow you to take out just $10,000 in student loans, is the more expensive school worth it in the quality of education you receive? Most of the time, the answer is no. I went to American University in Washington, D.C., as an undergrad, but my master's degree is from the not-so-famous Central Michigan University. Quite a few members of Congress got there without attending famous schools, as did those leading the world's biggest companies.

In Spencer Stuart's 2004 "Route to the Top" survey, the percentage of CEOs with Ivy League undergraduate degrees went from 19 percent in 1999 to only 10 percent in 2003.

Many successful students start out at a community college for two years, then transfer their credits to another school and receive a degree from that college.

This creates the hybrid effect of having a degree from a four-year institution, but also saving the money that would have been spent the first two years.

The education you receive is more important than the school name on your degree. My final piece of advice—when your child is about five, start teaching him or her the fight song from your state school.

• **Internet** •

www.ed.gov	*(Government guide to student loans)*
www.scholarships.com	*(Scholarship information)*
www.fastweb.com	*(Scholarship information)*
www.fafsa.ed.gov	*(Financial aid information)*

✳ Working and Saving ✳

I love it when teenagers work. I started working at age eleven, in the warehouse of a furniture store. I worked at the store during holidays and on weekends off and on through age fifteen. I swept the warehouse floor and carried accessories to customers' cars. When I was older, I worked on the delivery truck and unfortunately also worked on repossessions. I learned so much and made money at the same time.

The right age to work depends on your child and his motivation. But when he starts working, he will develop so many positives in his life. Whether the first job is baby-sitting, mowing lawns, raking leaves, planting flowers and plants, or being a lifeguard, your child will have a great feeling of achievement. For the first time in his life, he will feel truly empowered.

When your child starts working in a

regular workplace, usually a store or restaurant, he develops a bigger world view. He gets to meet people he wouldn't meet otherwise. In the best circumstances, he might meet a mentor who would give him a life-changing new perspective that brings out something great in him.

Working can teach kids some good lessons, including the value of saving for something he wants and what's expected of people in the workplace. Responsibility is a big lesson. With school, you as a parent make sure your kid gets to school on time, and the school lets you know if he's late or absent. That of course is not what the real world is like. A job teaches your child about consequences. You're expected to be at work on time, and you're expected to be there every day. If you're absent or late too often, you get fired. The positive reinforcement of small but frequent pay raises, and the negative reinforcement of being fired, is good for teenagers, as long as they don't work too much.

Working also is a good way to provide structure for kids who otherwise would have too much unstructured time, says Michael Popkin, president of Active Parenting Publishers (www.activeparenting .com), a company that produces video-based parenting education programs. Plus, some families simply need kids to work because there isn't enough money in the family budget to provide allowances.

I'm often asked how much work is right for a teen. I believe that twelve to fifteen hours a week during the school year is just about right. That would mean one weekend day and maybe one or two nights during the week or weekend.

Working too much can tire out a teenager and can interfere with other activities, such as sports and clubs. School and other activities should come first, but kids may focus on work and forget about school. Working at McDonald's is a lot easier than keeping up grades at school, so be careful to make sure work isn't interfering with schoolwork.

During the summer, up to twenty-five hours a week is great through age fifteen, and then thirty-five hours a week is appropriate for kids older than fifteen.

I've said very little so far about the money your son or daughter will earn, because that is not the most important part of the picture. I see your teen's first jobs as part of an exploration. Your child may see a potential career path open before her eyes. Something she learns in a part-time or summer job could lead to something she would love.

And for many teens, working at entry-level jobs has the opposite effect. Teens see that some part-time jobs could lead to a dead-end job path. This gives you an opportunity as a parent to talk to your child about her work experience and what she has learned from it. She'll tell you she doesn't want to work in the mailroom or be a fast-food cook for the rest of her life, and getting a good education is one of the best ways to make sure she can get a job that has more responsibility and higher pay.

Jaime Alpert, the daughter of Joni Alpert, who works on my radio show, told me that working as a teenager allowed her to earn money, get experience in the "real world," and become more involved in her community. Earning some money let Jaime and her twin sister, Lisa, feel less dependent on their parents and allowed them to save money to buy a car. Jaime and Lisa worked as babysitters during their high school years. Because they both had demanding course loads in school as well as sports and club activi-

ties, they restricted their babysitting to weekends. And because each babysitting job was separate, that gave them a lot of flexibility. They could turn down a job if they had to do homework or had some other obligation. Or one could fulfill a babysitting commitment while the other relaxed with friends. Since Jaime and Lisa are identical twins, that sometimes confused the children they tended, who must have wondered why the babysitter was named Lisa one night and Jaime another.

I've tried to encourage my older daughter, Rebecca, who's now fifteen, to take a job working for someone else, but she's making so much money as a babysitter that I can't get her to do it. One day she worked five hours at $10 an hour, making $50. It was her friend's birthday, so she and five other kids got together to rent a limo for her friend's birthday. She took the $50 babysitting job to pay for her share of the limo. Because there's a lot of demand for babysitters where we live, she's found she can make as much money as she wants. She turned down four babysitting jobs on one Friday night and took a fifth. She may not learn the lessons of working for someone else, but she's learning instead the rewards and responsibilities of being an entrepreneur, and that working for herself is something she enjoys. She's responsible for her own success and failure and for marketing her business. Rebecca took the initiative to make business cards for her babysitting business, using an online service called VistaPrint (www.vistaprint.com), which gives you 250 free business cards (you pay only for shipping) in hopes of selling you other products and services. Being an entrepreneur may be in our genes, because my two brothers, my sister, and I all run our own businesses.

Kids can also learn some great life skills by working. I had a call from a furious father whose sixteen-year-old son was working in an ice cream parlor. The owner would leave the kid alone in the store at night and expect him to close. To add insult to injury, the owner claimed that one night there was money missing from the cash drawer, so he deducted $100 from the young man's paycheck. The dad wanted to go to war on his son's behalf. After talking with the father, we put the son on the air, and talked with him about what rights he had and how to exercise them. I also advised him to

send a note to the ice cream parlor owner, saying he was contacting the government. Guess what the owner did? He paid the boy the disputed $100. The kid learned how to stand up for himself and the dad learned how capable his son is.

Incentives to Save

Your kids may earn a good deal of money working, especially during the summer, and you should give them incentives to save some of it. One great reason for a teenager to save money is to balance out the income they earn through the year. I talked to a thirteen-year-old who was making $40 a yard cutting lawns. He was going to make $600 a week over a ten-week summer, or $6,000. That's a gigantic amount of money for a thirteen-year-old. He wanted an iPod and called to ask me if he should buy it on eBay. (I told him no, to buy one new.) But then we started talking about saving money, which he hadn't thought about. I was worried that when the summer was over, he was going to consume that tremendous pile of money and have zero dollars left. By saving some of his summer earnings, he'd have money available if he wanted a CD or something during the year. It's like a squirrel that stores acorns to last through the winter, or a wise adult who keeps money in a rainy-day account. Your goal in talking to a teen about saving should be to help create some purpose, goals, and obligations, such as buying or maintaining a car. Use what a child wants as your teaching vehicle and your source of financial discipline. One of the ways you teach deferred gratification to a teen is to use a job as a springboard to teach the concept of saving—for his own car or insurance or maintenance on a car.

This summer job created the perfect opportunity for this thirteen-year-old to open a savings account and a Roth IRA, the first time in that child's life that money he earns is really relevant. As a parent, you should seize that opportunity and create three paths for that money: money the kid spends, money he saves for during the school year, and money he saves for the future. The easiest way to explain it to kids is you divide the money into three piles, one third to spend, one third for short-term savings, and one-third for long-term savings. You have to let your kids blow a certain amount of money. Adults blow money, too. Nobody

is going to be perfectly disciplined with every dollar they spend. When adults have a financial windfall, I actually encourage them to blow 10 percent of it. Do whatever you want to with it, to satisfy that need for immediate gratification. Then, use the other 90 percent to pay off debt or invest. Kids have no ongoing monthly obligations, unless they already have a car, so getting them to save two-thirds of what they make is not a real burden. At age fourteen and fifteen, the short-term savings can be for them to buy their own car, or a new iPod.

A great way to help your child save is to have her divert part of her paycheck into a savings account, if the employer offers a payroll deduction. If they don't, set up an automatic draft from the teen's checking account into a savings account. You can set up an account for your teen at www.ingdirect.com. It's easy for teens to log in and watch their money accrue interest.

My daughter Rebecca is fired up about an offer I made to her—she's working as a babysitter, and for every dollar she gives me to put into her new Roth IRA, I'll match it with a dollar. She thinks that's the coolest thing—that she's going to double her money. If I had said, "Rebecca, because you're earning money you're eligible to put some or all of it aside," she wouldn't have been interested. But when she knows I'll double the money she saves, it makes her think about whether she really needs to have the latest Beyoncé CD, or whether she wants to turn the $10 she would have spent on that CD into $20. It may sound like bribery, but many employers match contributions you make to your 401(k) account, and the government has a program where it will match retirement contributions for people who meet income eligibility requirements. This is the Daddy match. Now, the Roth is a retirement account, so the payoff is fifty years away for a fifteen-year-old. But when I told Rebecca about it, I told her I would double her money instantly. Then, after I had her attention, I told her what a Roth IRA is and how the money can be invested under the Roth IRA umbrella. She was interested because I made it relevant to her life. In doing that, I've done her an enormous favor, because if she develops the habit of deferring some amount of wants today in exchange for wealth in the future, she will benefit hugely. I showed her the chart from my book *Get Clark Smart* that shows how rich she can be if she starts saving money as a teenager (save $2,000 a year from age fifteen to twenty-two, and you'll have more than $1 million at age sixty-five), and she is so on board with this. It's funny, because Rebecca did not share my values at all about shopping for clothes, for example. She craves fashion and I buy clothes that are very inexpensive. But I was able to reach her with this message—save today and you will benefit in a big way later—and she got it. It doesn't mean that she won't want some particular designer brand of jeans, but she might get one pair instead of two. Or she might buy three CDs instead of six.

The beginning of your child's working life is a great time to talk about why you should save some of what you earn.

In a lot of families for many years, kids have had to work to help support the family. They weren't just expected to work, they *had* to work. Today, work is optional in many cases. And if a child has everything he wants, getting him motivated to work can be difficult. So you have to use a really tough stick. If they want money from you to do something, your answer is "No. There is no more money." If you have an unmotivated child, cut off the money when he turns sixteen. When summer comes, your son has to earn his own money. It may sound like tough love, but it works. If a child believes he can live off you, he will. If a child is lazy, why should he get up and go somewhere he doesn't want to be, when you'll give him what he wants anyway? So you take it away. If he sits around watching TV all day, disconnect the cable or satellite. If you revoke privileges and take the cash away, even if he's unmotivated, he has to get out of the house and work.

I've created a working contract for parents and teens to sign so each will know the other is serious about working.

• Internet •

www.activeparenting.com	(Parenting education)
www.ingdirect.com	(Online savings account)
www.vistaprint.com	(Free business cards)

✳ Jobs ✳

It's a very unusual teenager who knows exactly what he or she wants to do when she grows up. Kids generally haven't thought through what jobs they would enjoy, what those jobs pay, and what level of education such jobs might require. I want you to help them think about these issues now.

Start by talking with your teen about what kind of things she might enjoy doing, and use that as a springboard to talk about what kind of money different jobs might represent. Most engineering jobs are near the top of the earning power scale. Nursing is a solid-paying career. Truck driving is a perennial.

One thing that's very important to teach your teen is the relationship between education and earning power. Over

Working Contract

I _____ on this _____ day of _____ , 20___ , do agree to the stipulations stated below regarding the privilege of working at a part-time job. I will abide by the rules of this "working contract," outlined below.

I will take a part-time job that requires me to work no more than _____ hours per week.

I understand that this job is not to interfere with my schoolwork. If at any time my average falls below _____ , or I receive any grade below _____ , I will then have to give my employer two weeks' written notice and terminate my employment.

I will put at least _____% of my earnings into a Roth IRA each month. My parents/guardians will provide a _____% match to my contribution.

If my parent/guardian provides transportation to and from this job, I will assist by paying _____ as compensation for gas and mileage each week.

If I decide that I do not want to work at this job anymore, I will give my employer ample time to find a replacement. This includes giving at least two weeks' written notice, and then showing responsibility by working in good faith until my last stated shift.

I have read the above agreement and agree to the stipulations.

Signed on this _____ day of _____ , 20____.

_____ Teenager

_____ Parent and/or Guardian

_____ Parent and/or Guardian

the course of an American worker's life, someone with a high school diploma can expect to earn $1.2 million, according to the U.S. Census Bureau. But the financial rewards grow with higher education, as you can see in this chart:

Degree	Expected lifetime earnings (Ages 25–64, according to U.S. Census Bureau 2000 census)
High school diploma	$1.2 million
Bachelor's degree	$2.1 million
Master's degree	$2.5 million
Doctorate degree	$3.4 million
Professional degree*	$4.4 million

*Men with professional degrees will accumulate $2 million more than their female counterparts.
(Source: U.S. Department of Commerce, Census Bureau)

With these conversations, you start to create a matrix in your child's mind about the relationship between education, income, and his interests. Your teen might think, "If I get this level of education, that will allow me to do any of these things. Now which of these things would I enjoy?" Jobs and careers shouldn't be just about money. People should do things they enjoy, and that would allow them a certain level of income. If you've already talked to your teen about what houses and cars cost, that raises the question of how much he would need to earn to achieve the lifestyle he wants, and which careers would provide that kind of income. If he can't generate the income he wants with an undergraduate degree, that might mean going to graduate school.

Kids should understand that their wants need to be realistic, based on what the average person makes. I still have some work to do with Rebecca to get her where she needs to be before she leaves the nest, and all kids are works in progress. There are lots of things she gets, but still some she doesn't. She's getting better at understanding relative value and consumption. What she doesn't get is what kind of career she'd have to

What People Earn

Job	Median pay
College not required:	
Pilot	$109,580 a year
Loan officer	$43,980 a year
Funeral director	$43,380 a year
Mail carrier	$39,530 a year
Executive secretary/administrative assistant	$33,410 a year
Customer service representative	$26,240 a year
Electrician	$19.90 an hour
Carpenter	$16.44 an hour
Truck driver	$15.97 an hour
Painter	$13.98 an hour
College degree:	
Computer/Information systems manager	$85,240 a year
Chemical engineer	$72,490 a year
Business executive	$68,210 a year
Computer programmer	$60,290 a year
Architect	$56,620 a year
Advanced degree:	
Dentist	$123,210 a year
Lawyer	$90,290 a year
Pharmacist	$77,050 a year
Psychologist	$51,170 a year
Registered nurse	$48,090 a year
Librarian	$43,090 a year

have to accommodate her level of consumption.

Let's say the estimated mortgage payment is $1,250 a month. To afford that payment, you'd want to earn four times that, or $5,000 a month. That's $60,000 a year. Kids get paid by the hour, so you could translate that to $28.85 an hour ($60,000/52 weeks/40 hours a week). A kid making $6 an hour can see that they won't be able to pay that mortgage on what they currently earn.

If you have a child who doesn't think college is important, you can show him the kind of money he can earn in jobs that don't require a college degree. Carpenters, for example, earned a median hourly wage of $16.44 in 2002, according to the U.S. Labor Department's Bureau of Labor Statistics. That's a little more than $34,000 a year, based on a forty-hour workweek. Electricians had a median hourly wage of $19.90.

Having a skill is a key to good earnings for many jobs that don't require a college degree. For many kids, going to a two-year technical school instead of college may be a good choice.

You may or may not want to tell your children what you earn. Sometimes parents clam up when kids reach a stage, usually in middle school or junior high, when they ask how much money each parent makes. The parents will say it's none of their business, which builds a wall and then it's over. You've delivered the message that money is something you're not going to talk about. Some parents are worried that their kids will tell their friends what they make, and then that information will be spread throughout their neighborhood. And that is a risk. Kids may brag about what their parents make, or use it as a way to compare their parents with their friends' parents. It may be easier for people who work for the government, because government workers have specific GS grades that determine their pay. The military is similar, and union workers also can't be private about their pay. But for the rest of us, what we earn is a closely guarded secret.

My advice is to tell your children what you make if you think they can be responsible with that information. If you feel comfortable sharing information about your pay with them, you won't believe how valuable it can be. In addition to telling your children what you make, you should show them where it all goes—how much goes to federal and state income taxes (if your state has an income tax) and to Social Security and Medicare taxes, and how much goes to major family expenses such as rent or the mortgage, food, car payments, and utilities. You may risk a loss of privacy, but the lessons your child learns will be invaluable.

✳ Saving on Clothes, Music, and Movies ✳

Clothes

Just as I advise adults to look for the best deals when they spend money, I believe teens should do the same.

One of the best ways for teens to save on clothes is to concentrate on style, not on brand names. There are so many good designer knockoffs now that it's easy for teens to be stylish and look as good as their friends, and also spend a lot less money on their clothes. Don't think your teen will be convinced? Take her to a high-end department store and walk through the store without buying anything. Then go to a discount shoe store, such as Payless or Designer Shoe Warehouse, and you'll find some great copies of the high-fashion merchandise. For example, Payless has copies of Nine West styles.

Target, Kmart, and even Wal-Mart have some really cool clothes. No one will ever know where your teen got them, and he or she will look great. Wal-Mart has a clothing line called George, which is one of the top clothing lines in England. Wal-Mart got it in an overseas ac-quisition and brought it to the United States. Nobody knows this stuff is there, but it's right there inside Wal-Mart, displayed badly. You'll find very fashion-forward items for $10 that you'd expect to pay $60 for elsewhere.

Thrift stores are another great place for your teen to save money on clothes. Take her to a high-end thrift store such as those run by the Junior League, and you'll find great nearly new clothes at great prices. Some may still have the tags on. Rebecca got a pair of Seven jeans, which normally sell for $150 and up, for $10 at a thrift store. Your teen can score big-time by knowing what the fashions are but refusing to pay full price.

Designer Shoe Warehouse also is a great place for boys to buy their athletic shoes. They have a lot of variety at great prices. Discount stores such as Marshalls and T.J. Maxx also have lots of designer shoes and clothes at low prices.

Some kids are going to have to have the Nike "swoosh" on their shoes. Others are okay with the look. Your job is to convince your teen that the marketers are trying to con them by making them pay outrageous prices for a high-end brand.

Adults have become more sophisticated about buying off-brands and store brands, so marketers have turned their attention to teens, even preteens, and found a prime market, which doesn't seem to be based on family income. Adolescents want to fit in so badly that they're vulnerable to the pressures of doing what the popular kids are doing. And the popular kids are wearing Lucky jeans and carrying Prada bags.

The over-the-top desire among teens for brand names started about fifteen years ago, when department stores started having trouble differentiating themselves from one another. Every store was carrying the same clothing from the same designers, which made the clothing a commodity. That allowed consumers to shop the store that had the best sale. So the department stores started to heavily promote their own private labels, to differentiate themselves and gain power from the designers. Instead, retailers conditioned adults to look for the quality of goods, instead of the labels, and to look for the best prices. So designers shifted their focus to teens and preteens,

or "tweens," and created a big new market for themselves.

One way that I've dealt with this is to let Rebecca buy brand-name products if she can find them at a deep discount. I let her buy a $90 designer warm-up outfit that was on sale at Sam's Club for $19, because it helped her understand value. As a parent, you might prefer your child never buy clothing like this. But you also have to decide when to compromise.

Music

A great way to save money on CDs is to buy them used. Because of the popularity of MP3 players, CDs are becoming less relevant. So your teen can buy used CDs cheap, usually for $6 to $8 each. A used CD will sound as good as a new one, as long as it isn't damaged.

Also, because of a federal antitrust court ruling, new CDs are a lot cheaper than they used to be, if you shop around.

Last, your teen can skip the CD, as many people are, and buy the music she wants online. If you have a teen who's really into music, talk to her about buying a monthly subscription instead of paying per song for downloads. For a flat rate of $7 to $10 a month, or about the cost of one used CD, your teen can listen to virtually any song she wants to, at any time. You can't burn copies of the songs or save them on a portable music device, but you can listen from any computer, laptop, desktop, or ultra-portable Internet device. Services include iTunes (www.apple.com/itunes), Rhapsody (www.rhapsody.com), and Music Match (www.musicmatch.com).

If your teen really wants to be able to burn copies of songs onto CDs, she can legally download songs for less than $1, about what you and I used to pay for an old 45 RPM record.

Some independent musicians make their music available for free on the Web, either on their own Web sites or on independent music sites such as www.epitonic.com, www.audiostreet.net, and www.ubl.com.

Although this landscape changes often, there are many sites at which you can legally download music for free, with permission from the artist. Two such sites are www.limewire.com and www.iuma.com.

• Internet •

www.apple.com/itunes	*(Pay-per-song music downloads)*
www.audiostreet.net	*(Free music downloads from independent artists)*
www.epitonic.com	*(Free music downloads from independent artists)*
www.iuma.com	*(Free music downloads)*
www.limewire.com	*(Free music downloads)*
www.musicmatch.com	*(Pay-per-song music downloads)*
www.rhapsody.com	*(Pay-per-song music downloads)*
www.ubl.com	*(Free music downloads from independent artists)*

Movies

If your teen really likes movies, it's a good idea to join one of the movie subscription services, such as Netflix or one of its competitors, rather than going to the movie theater or renting movies one at a time.

And just as buying used CDs is a good value, so is buying used DVDs. Your teen can buy a used DVD, and watch it over and over, for about what he would pay for one theater ticket. And the popcorn is a whole lot cheaper at home.

If your teen always wants to see the newest movies at the theater, why not save on theater tickets? If you or your teen is a member of AAA, you can buy discount tickets there. You can also buy discount movie tickets from the warehouse clubs, although most tickets are for a particular theater chain.

Go to the Web sites of the theater chain closest to your home and look with your son or daughter to see what discounts are available. The chains often offer coupons for discounts on tickets, as well as on the overpriced concessions. So instead of being way, way overpriced, they're just way overpriced.

One thing some theater chains are doing is selling passes for unlimited visits. If your teen goes to the movies several times a month, check to see if any theater around you has a flat-rate pass. That certainly beats the cost of buying tickets each time.

Concessions are a good way to teach something important to your teen. Since my children were young, I always made sure they were well fed and well hydrated before we went to a sporting event. And they knew I wasn't going to buy anything inside the stadium. They learned early on how much you can be forced to pay when you're a captive and that I had a zero tolerance rule for that. Movie theaters price like stadiums do. I don't believe in sneaking candy in, and I don't believe you should teach kids to break the rules. But you can eat and drink before you go in, and eat and drink after you leave. This is just advice, though. If your kids want to take $10 and get one bucket of popcorn and one soft drink, they can. Or they can do those things outside the theater for $2. Would they rather have $8 still in their hands than spend the $10? If it's the kids' own money, they're more attuned to the concept you're trying to teach. And if it's your money, give them the $10 and let them decide. They can spend it or keep the change.

Another option is to talk to your teen about going to the 5:30 P.M. movie, which often is discounted, instead of the 7:30 P.M., which is full price. Instead of eating dinner and then going to the movie, he could go to the movie and eat dinner afterward. Your teen may roll his eyes at you when you suggest things like this, but he hears you. It's part of communicating, in little and big ways, that money is finite and that he should want to get maximum value out of each dollar. Even if you can't motivate your teen by the idea that he can spend less, you may succeed by pointing out that spending less means he can go twice for the same money. You get more for your money.

✳ Saving for the Prom ✳

One of the strangest changes in our culture in the last twenty years is what a prom or high school dance represents to kids and the spending that goes with it. Proms used to be a nice but very basic event. The boy would rent a tuxedo, and the girl might get an inexpensive new dress, or borrow one. Today many children treat a prom as a coronation, a festive occasion whose cost can hit $1,000 per couple. Among the things that have become common are stretch limousines, very fancy dinners, and hotel suites for after-parties. And it seems that each year, they get larger and larger.

We were having dinner at a very high-end steak house for a relative's birthday, and it happened to be right in the middle of prom season. One stretch limo after another pulled up to the restaurant. The teenagers got out of the limos and ate $80-a-person meals at the restaurant. All the girls were in dresses to die for, and the guys were in exotic designer tuxedos.

Not all teenagers are into having a lavish prom. Last prom season, I put a teenager on the air to tell a great story. This group of teens had decided to rebel against the materialism of the prom. They weren't going to do the over-the-top prom, so they rode public transportation to the dance, used coupons to save money at a restaurant, and wore hand-me-down clothes. They looked absolutely fine and had a great time, while spending almost no money at all.

I realize that you don't want to spoil

your child's fun, but because everyone can relate to the prom, it's a great way to teach the value of money. You can buy a tuxedo now for $100, rather than rent it. You can get a prom dress at a discount store for less than $100. You can rent a nice black car instead of a limo. I heard one story about a junior prom in which a few responsible seniors got together and, in order to make some money, borrowed their parents' nice cars, wore tuxedo shirts with shorts and sunglasses, and drove the juniors to their prom. It was cool for the juniors because the seniors were driving them, but they didn't spend nearly the money they would have on a limo. (The seniors were from the Mothers Against Drunk Driving group, so safety was emphasized.)

Your teenager and her friends can meet at someone's house for a dinner party instead of going to a luxury restaurant, or have a picnic in the park or at the beach. According to the Web site www.promadvice.com, "A lot of prom groups are opting for fun over fancy."

There are so many ways that you can create a sense of value in the prom budget, and set in your teen's mind a sense of priorities and the value of a dollar, versus blowing all that cash on one night. For some reason, as parents, we believe that if you spend all that money, you're creating a more special night for your teenager. But I don't think you create something special out of spending.

One way to help your teen establish a sense of priorities is to agree to pay a certain amount of money toward prom expenses, maybe $200. If your teen wants to spend more, he can earn it and save it in his own "prom fund." Have this discussion very early in the school year. Don't wait until spring. You can use this to encourage delayed gratification, saving for a goal, and budgeting, among other financial skills. Your values may not include spending several hundred dollars on a meal. But if that's really important to your son, let him have six months to save up for that meal.

• **Internet** •

www.promadvice.com   (Saving money on the prom)

✳ Investing ✳

My father taught me to read the stock tables when I was in elementary school. He had worked on the floor of the New York Stock Exchange as a young man, and he had a lifelong fascination with investments and stocks. He wasn't very good at money management itself, but he knew about investing, and it was fantastic for me. I knew what price-earnings ratios were before I knew how to do algebra, and it's helped me throughout my life.

Sometimes it's hard for adults to explain some basic investment terms to children. If you want to teach a child what stock is, try this analogy. Say you own an ice cream store, which means you own 100 percent of the stock. But let's say you want to have a chain of ice cream stores, and you don't have enough money to own that many stores, even though you're running a good business and making money. So you ask other people if they want to join you in opening more stores. You give them part ownership by selling them stock. If the company has 100 shares of stock and you own five shares, you own 5 percent of the

company. Large corporations have many shareholders. When I checked, McDonald's Corp. had a total value of nearly $36 billion, and nearly three-quarters of its shares were owned by mutual funds, pension funds, and other institutional shareholders. If you bought shares in one of those mutual funds, you would own a tiny piece of McDonald's.

If the owners don't want to own less of the company, they can get money by selling bonds. A bond is basically an IOU, a piece of paper that says you're going to give me $100, and in return I'm going to pay you back over the years the $100, plus interest. It's like a loan, but from a company instead of the bank.

When many people buy stocks or bonds, they don't buy the actual stock or bonds from the company. Instead, they buy from a mutual fund, in which a lot of people put their money together to buy pieces of a basket full of stocks and/or bonds. As part of a group, you can afford to own a small piece of many different companies, which is safer than owning shares in one company or a few companies. You couldn't do that on your own unless you were Bill Gates.

You can involve your son or daughter in investing by buying shares of a stock or bond mutual fund, then follow the progress of your investments online or in monthly statements. But the most important thing is to teach your child to set aside something for the future. If you live your life by spending everything you have, you're like a tightrope walker at a circus, balancing on a thin wire and trying not to fall. If you don't set some money aside for the future, it's like walking the tightrope without a net to catch you if you fall. Without a financial safety net, you're always one misstep away from serious trouble.

The Stock Market Game

There's a terrific way for your child to learn about investing in the stock market. Many schools around the country participate in the Stock Market Game, which is operated by the Securities Industry Foundation for Economic Education in New York. Twice a year, students get the chance to pretend to be investors. Each group of students gets $100,000 in pretend money

to invest. At the end of ten weeks, the team with the most money wins. Guided by their teachers, students learn to buy and sell stocks, and see what it's like to invest. They learn how to do basic research—to see whether companies they are interested in are profitable or are losing money, whether their annual sales are growing or shrinking, and whether the price of the company's stock has been rising or falling.

In bull markets and bear markets, students have learned about investing and had fun doing it. There's more information available about the Stock Market Game at www.smgww.org.

If your child's school doesn't participate in the Stock Market Game, or if you prefer something less formal, you can play at home. Use play money to buy stocks and track your progress online or in the newspaper to see how your portfolio is doing. You could buy $10,000 worth of stock, let your son or daughter buy $10,000 worth, and play against each other—see who is doing better each month. Talk about why the companies you or your child picked are doing well, poorly, or about average.

Getting Involved

A few years ago, there were a number of programs from the brokerage houses that were designed to help parents get children to begin investing, in a way that would both build their money and teach them about investing. But there are only a few I know about that are still geared toward kids. One that I like is USAA's First Start Fund. If you are setting up the account for your child, then the minimum investment is only $250. If you are going to set up a monthly investment of $20 or more, then there is no initial deposit. But if you aren't going to set up a monthly plan, then the minimum is $3,000. If you are setting up an IRA, the minimum is $2,000. To sign up, call 1-800-531-0553. There is also the Columbia Young Investor Fund, which used to be called the Stein-Roe Young Investor Fund, but I don't recommend that you invest in this fund, because the fees are too high and the company was involved in the mutual fund trading scandal. But the fund's Web site, www.younginvestor.com, has some great information that can help young people learn about investing. The site has information on how to plan, how to invest, how the stock market works and how a company goes public. And the information is geared toward kids, teens, and adults.

Mutual funds used to have accounts that allowed you to start with $500 and make contributions of as little as $25 a month. Now most require $1,000 to start and minimum deposits of $50 a month. That's a taller order for kids. You could open the account with your money, or some of your money, or keep your child's money in a savings account until she has enough to open a mutual fund account.

The important thing with children and teens isn't to get the best return on your investment, but to teach them that you should spend less than you earn, and put some of your earnings aside for the future. One very simple way to do that, especially with younger children, is through savings bonds. You can buy a savings bond for as little as $50. So if your child can save as little as $25 from her allowance, and you match it with another $25, she'll have enough for a $50 savings bond. (Savings bonds used to be sold at a discount from their face value, so you'd buy a $100 savings bond for $50 and eventually it would be worth $100. Now they're sold at face value.) A savings bond can't be cashed in for a year, so your child will be committed to the investment. The U.S. Treasury has a Web site that teaches kids about U.S. Savings Bonds, complete with games. The Web address is www.publicdebt.treas.gov/sav/savkids.htm. Buy savings bonds at www.savingsbonds.gov.

A great mutual fund to open for your child is Vanguard's STAR Fund. It will help your child learn about investing, and he can easily add money to it through the years. I love Vanguard STAR because it offers complete diversification in one investment. It puts money into a variety of stocks, a variety of bonds, and a little bit of money in cash. As your child gets older and he chooses to learn, he'll learn just from this that he can invest in big companies or small companies, and that he can invest internationally. The explanation that comes with the fund is so great that I think a sophomore in high school could read it and understand what's going on. It also has a super-low expense ratio of 0.4 percent. In addition, the Vanguard Web site has some great general information about investing.

If you have a teenager who's working, I'd recommend you invest in a fund like Vanguard STAR, but do it within a Roth IRA. Your teen won't be able to access the money until retirement, but then all the money will be hers tax-free. Give your child extra incentive, as I did, by matching every dollar she puts into her account with a dollar of yours. She'll double her money instantly, then watch it grow tax-free.

You can show your teen how money grows by using your own retirement account as an example. Log in to your retirement account on the Web and show her the growth you've had over the last few years. Explain the concept of dollar-cost averaging, which is putting the same amount of money into your investment account at the same time each month. If the market goes up, your portfolio grows. If it goes down, your monthly contribution buys you more shares of stock. Over the long term, you gain.

The *Los Angeles Times* has a great online course about investing called Investing 101. Take the course online with your teen at www.latimes.com/money.

Another fun way to learn about investing is to form a family investing club. You and your teen contribute a small amount of money each month. Each member of the club gets an equal say in how the money is invested. It makes the teen feel empowered. You can teach your teen how to evaluate a company or mutual fund, or learn with him at the same time.

I'm not big on buying individual stocks for kids, because it's so inefficient to buy a single share of stock. But one Web site that makes this possible is www.sharebuilder.com, which allows you to own individual stocks very cheaply. They do a bulk buy once a week, where they pool all their customers' purchases. A similar site is www.buyandhold.com.

You could also check the top ten stocks owned by the mutual fund and look for companies your child might be familiar with—she might like to own a little bit of McDonald's or Disney. Then you can have the company's annual report sent to you, with all the great photographs and charts, and involve your teen in the experience of being a part owner of a giant corporation. Just go to the company's Web site and request an investor information kit. The kit will include the company's most recent annual report, as well as other information on its recent sales and profits, plus general company information.

The Jump$tart Coalition

Another great place for kids to learn about investing is the Jump$tart Coalition for Personal Financial Literacy (www.jumpstart.org), which offers lessons for elementary, middle, and high school students on financial strategies such as budgeting, managing credit, philanthropy, and home ownership.

The Jump$tart Coalition also has some fun tools, such as a Jump$tart Reality Check that lets young people pick what kind of lifestyle they want and how much it will cost them. There's also an interesting list, "12 Principles That Every Young Person Should Know": map your financial future; don't expect something for nothing; high returns equal high risks; know your take-home pay; compare interest rates; pay yourself first; money doubles by the "Rule of 72"; your credit past is your credit future; start saving young; stay insured; budget your money; and don't borrow what you can't repay.

● **Internet** ●

www.buyandhold.com	*(Buy individual stocks inexpensively)*
www.jumpstart.org	*(Jump$tart Coalition for Personal Financial Literacy)*
www.latimes.com/money	*(Investing 101 online course)*
www.publicdebt.treas.gov/sav/savkids.htm	*(Learn about savings bonds)*
www.savingsbonds.gov	*(U.S. savings bonds)*
www.sharebuilder.com	*(Buy individual stocks inexpensively)*
www.smgww.org	*(Stock Market Game)*
www.younginvestor.com	*(Investor information for kids)*
www.vanguard.com	*(Information about the Vanguard STAR Fund)*
www.usaa.com	*(Information about USAA's First Start Fund)*

✳ Ripoffs That Target Your Teens ✳

There are all kinds of scams aimed at adults, from time shares to fake contests to phony charities, and now there are a growing number aimed at your kids. I'm going to tell you about a few, and give you an idea how to teach your teens to avoid them.

One of the worst, and most expensive, is the overpriced trade school. Would your kid like to produce songs for top recording artists? Would she like to direct music videos? All it will take, say these scammers, is for her to enroll at their trade school, for the staggering price of $35,000 for one year of tuition. Kids are only too eager to pay for a chance to work in the

glamorous music business. Kids often will borrow the money themselves under the federal student loan program to attend these schools. Even if the government determines the school has an unusually high default rate and takes away student-loan rights, the kids still are required to pay back the money they borrowed.

These schools do provide training, but it's a long way from there to a job. If getting the coveted job is unlikely, it obviously doesn't make sense to pay that kind of money for a year of trade school. But kids already are presold on this, and it's not hard for a slick recruiter to reel them in. They always have pictures of people in limousines, and many teenagers believe in the stretch limousine as a symbol of celebrity and success in life.

The trade school scam is aimed at the 73 percent of all kids who don't graduate from traditional colleges and who think they're headed for dull dead-end jobs. They leap at the chance to work behind the scenes, for big salaries, in a glamorous business.

I had a call recently from a fellow who's raising his nephew, and the nephew really wanted to go to one of these very expensive schools. The uncle asked me whether it was a good idea, and if not, how could he have a discussion with his nephew about it? As I talked with him, we typed the name of the school into an online search engine. The school's site came up first, along with a couple of propaganda sites. Then came dozens of gripes, by people with bitter complaints about the school. It's always good to read the complaints and let all that unhappiness bring a giddy teen back to reality. Have your child do the research himself, or do it with him. Have him type the name of the school you're looking at into your favorite search engine, and see what comes up.

Another way to discuss this with your child is to call a recording studio in your city or another city. Again, do it together or have your child make the call. Ask to speak to a recording engineer if one is available, or get the name of one and call back. Ask them how they learned the business and got started. What you'll find is that a lot of those people didn't go to school at all, or went to a traditional four-year college. They may have gotten their jobs through luck or word-of-mouth, or just fundamental hard work. I see this all the time at the radio station where I work. There are people working there who didn't go to college, along with others who went to four-year colleges to study communications or broadcasting.

If your kids want to acquire skills for a particular industry, the first place to start is a state-supported technical college. It's not going to be glamorous, but they'll learn the skills and they'll do it nearly for free. Tuition is very low.

Modeling Scams

Another high-glamour scam that targets kids is modeling road shows. These folks come to your town, rent a hotel ballroom, and run a bunch of ads inviting people to come down for a chance to get into the modeling business. Hundreds of people, up to a thousand, will come, and they'll see slides and videos showing the glamour of the modeling industry. The kids watch with stars in their eyes.

Generally, an interviewing process follows, then a selection. They send home a certain number of people and ask the rest to stay. To the group that's "made the first cut," the process seems even more credible. Eventually comes the push to sign your child up for some kind of modeling agency program. In the most common, you're told that, after you've paid the fee, your child will have a chance to be reviewed by "top people" with agencies in the "top markets" for modeling. Who knows who those clowns are that they bring in? But it's not a legitimate way for anybody to get into modeling. All that happens is the child's hopes are dashed and the parent is poorer. Check www.modelingscams.org or www. actorsource.com for some good info on avoiding these scams.

Any so-called modeling agency that wants to charge you anything is lying to you and cheating you. In the legitimate modeling industry, the agency makes money from its clients' work by taking a commission on the revenue they generate. The only money someone should lay out is for pictures, and those are done by a photographer who shoots composite cards, or "comp cards," which consist of one color shot on the front and multiple shots on the back. They're not done by the agency, so anybody who offers a one-stop shop is lying.

Modeling scams sometimes involve modeling classes, offered by either phony agencies or by specialized modeling schools that claim they are going to get your child work, after she graduates, as a model. Many of these people end up as "presenters" at trade shows or conventions, handing out brochures or free samples of some company's products, or tackling customers at a department store and spraying perfume on them. It's not glamorous and it doesn't pay much. The truth is that modeling is one of the most difficult fields for someone to break into.

One of the best ways to get involved in acting or modeling is to take classes at a local community theater. Community theater flourished in the late 1990s, and many more theaters began offering classes to supplement their income. Classes are not expensive, usually $60 to $90 per course (6–10 sessions), and students will pick up a lot of the desired skills and poise.

Student Trips

There are dozens of organizations that say their mission is student enrichment, but their real business is to make money by selling expensive student trips. They make their pitch to you directly, or to your son or daughter, that the teen has been chosen as one of a select few, because either their school or community has determined them to be individuals of outstanding potential and achievement. Therefore, as one of this elite group, the teen has the opportunity to join others on an exclusive trip to one of the nation's or world's outstanding political or cultural destinations. The letters are all very congratulatory, and they emphasize the exclusivity of these trips and what great opportunities they are. Kids and their parents are often amazingly excited, until they see how much the trips cost—they're very expensive, from $2,500 to $9,000.

Many of the trips go to Washington, D.C., and the organizers claim that your child will have access to top briefings from very important Washington officials. That is a gross exaggeration of the agendas for these trips. I'm a big believer in kids' being exposed to Washington, D.C., and the branches of government and having an opportunity to travel overseas—all great eye-openers for a child. But it's nonsense that these trips are exclusive or that the kids are getting some kind of extraspecial opportunity. What I find when I talk to parents is they're being pressured by their kids because all their friends are going on the trip. I recommend that parents talk to their teens and tell them they could take a similar trip as a family, and two, three, or four people could go for about the same cost as these organizations would charge for just your son or daughter to take one of these trips. Go online with your teen and look at the cost of airfares and hotels. In the case of trips to Washington, D.C., you could call your congressman or senator's office. They arrange for all kinds of access to various government buildings and agencies, as a way of trying to keep constituents happy, and it's all free. As you do this research, you may find that the real reason your teen wants to go is to take a junket with his buddies. If that's what it's about, make him an offer. You could pay what you estimate the trip to be worth, based on your research, and if your teen wants to go, he can use his savings or work to come up with the rest. Then your teen can decide how much it's worth it to go.

As far as Europe goes, a much better alternative for your child is to wait until college, and then take advantage of one of the many school programs that allows students to spend junior year overseas, taking classes and earning credits in France, England, or wherever, with the approval of their school. Students don't have to transfer in or out; the semester abroad, arranged by the college, benefits both schools. The home school receives some money, yet has more space to enroll another student, so it's almost double-dipping. Study abroad programs have become very popular, and they're a great idea.

Another danger of these student trips is that organizers sometimes will take money from you and then go bust. De-posits normally must be paid well in advance, usually by check or cash, and if the operator fails to deliver the trip, the money is gone. Unless the operator proves that they have posted a performance bond, you have no way of knowing whether your money will be safe. Other groups actually have been on the trip, away in Mexico, when the tour operator failed. I talked with one group that was stuck in Mexico, with no way to get home. They couldn't even find a place to stay. The hotel they were supposed to stay in said they didn't have reservations, and several other hotels rejected them. It was a nightmare. They had to scramble to buy replacement tickets at the last minute, at very high cost.

One way to protect yourself and your child would be to buy travel insurance. There's a Web site, www.insuremytrip .com, that allows you to buy travel insurance from a variety of companies.

The student trips are similar to another ripoff for students, in which students are supposedly selected to appear in an exclusive *Who's Who* book. For $79 or so, students will get a vanity book that very few people will ever see. It's too expensive for the limited value you get.

• Internet •

www.actorsource.com   *(Avoiding acting scams)*
www.insuremytrip.com   *(Buying travel insurance)*
www.modelingscams.org   *(Avoiding modeling scams)*

✳ Games for Teens ✳

www.orangekids.com

Not to be outdone by Fleet, ING Direct has a great kids-only Web site that brings kids "around a money world" to learn about saving. It's great for teaching complicated concepts to preteens and teens, such as currency exchange, supply and demand, and budgeting and spending. It has a great quiz, with a built-in calculator, to teach the relative value of money.

www.treas.gov/kids

A word scramble and word search games teach teens basic savings terminology.

www.moneyopolis.com

Moneyopolis is a great interactive tutor with neat graphics to teach teens about priorities and money. Examples include saving for a first prom or school trip. It grades teens as they go along, so as they're doing something, they get a feel for whether they're getting the concept.

www.zillions.org

I know it's weird to talk about something that failed, but Zillions.org, which was *Consumer Reports'* effort to target kids, is still on the Web. Its product tests are obviously outdated and worthless, but the information about money is evergreen and very well done. They do a good job teaching about the stock market, about money in general, and about brand names versus off-brand. It's not very interactive, but the lessons are great.

• **Top Tips for Your Teen** •

○ Teens have the ability to earn money beyond their allowances, so the allowance you give them is just a base.

○ Teach your child to save some of his allowance by offering to double whatever allowance he has left every six months or at the end of the year.

○ Debit cards are a great teaching tool for teenagers, because they can spend only what's in the account.

○ Talk with your children about what houses, apartments, and cars cost.

○ When she reaches tenth grade, talk to your child about what can happen if you abuse credit.

○ Take your teen to a high-end department store and walk through the store without buying anything. Then go to a discount store and look for similar styles.

○ Instead of buying CDs or downloading songs, consider a subscription service that lets your teen listen to virtually any song, any time, for one monthly fee.

○ Working can teach kids good lessons, including the value of saving for something they want and what's expected of people in the workplace.

○ Don't buy your teenager a new car. Buy him a clunker or make him buy his own clunker. Then, make him pay for the insurance, gas, oil changes, and other maintenance.

○ Involve your teenager in investing by buying shares of a stock or bond mutual fund, then follow the progress of his investments online or in monthly statements.

CHAPTER 3

Adult Children

Our perception of adulthood has changed so much since the baby boom generation came along. Years ago, kids who turned eighteen were cast loose and their parents wished them a nice life. Children went to work and they were on their own, able to establish their own lives.

But now that almost 30 percent of kids graduate from college, and many others attend college at least for a while, the transition from childhood to adulthood has become very fuzzy. When a child becomes an adult is not at the point of a first job, or going to college. A tremendous number of kids in their twenties—and I say "kids in their twenties" on purpose—are boomeranging back into their parents' households. Kids who move out, then move back home. There are kids who are in school, out of school, in work, out of work. So the rules of the game aren't clear and simple, like they may have been when you were growing up. I saw one report that put the end of adolescence at age twenty-four.

This hazy end to childhood has been difficult on parents and children, raising tough questions. When they move back home, do these not-quite-adults have to live by house rules? Do they have to follow a curfew? Do they have to clean their rooms? Do they pay rent?

Even if these young people are living on their own, they may be burdened by student loans or credit card debt, or they may be earning low entry-level wages. If they need a car to get to work, they may ask Mom or Dad to co-sign a car loan. All of these issues are tying parents to their children beyond what would seem a normal age, and in ways that can be very messy. If you do continue to feed money to your children in their twenties, are they going to be able to achieve independence, or are they always going to be on the parental dole?

Dealing with these challenges requires more thinking on your part, and more communicating back and forth with your adult children about your expectations and theirs. You want to ensure that you don't feel taken advantage of and that you're not holding them back from moving on with their lives.

In this section I'll talk about how you can help your children in a way that will guide them toward financial independence, instead of further dependence on you.

✳ Helping Twenty-Something Kids ✳

By the time your child reaches his twenties, he has options and choices that people didn't use to have at that age. Twenty-somethings potentially could have multiple lines of credit—to a department store, an electronics store, a furniture store, and a general purpose credit card. They can usually obtain car loans. Even a home loan is possible in many cases for someone in their early twenties.

The hard part for people that age is calibrating all that freedom, so that they don't get in over their heads. Many twenty-somethings seem to have an almost automatic sense about this. They have the ability to handle money very well, even with what seems to be unlimited freedom. Others may be able to handle it well, but because they're just starting out, they may need some transitional help from parents. Still others may be predisposed, when given access to so much credit, to borrowing too much.

As a parent, you have to know your own children, know when it's best to help them. Some kids will never ask for help. With the others, you have to think carefully, and with your head, not your heart, decide whether you're helping them by giving them a boost that they need or hurting them by giving them yet another chance to borrow. The goal is to help your children establish financial independence, not to do things that may make them more dependent on you.

I had the privilege of talking recently with a listener who is twenty-four years old and who already owns her own home and is putting 15 percent of her pay into her 401(k) plan. Her question to me was what to do with the extra $300 a month she had. She had no debt other than her mortgage and some student loans she was close to paying off, having used them to put herself through college. That's a twenty-four-year-old who has established herself with great independence and spends far below her income. That young adult has already developed great habits. Maybe her parents taught her to be that way, or maybe

it came naturally. But she and others like her—they get it.

Figuring out what to do depends on your son or daughter. If your daughter is a responsible person who earned A's in college but is having trouble paying the bills on an entry-level salary, it's fine to help provide a financial bridge to true independence. My coauthor used to work with a young woman whose parents helped her with her rent during her early twenties. Now she's in her early thirties, has a great job, and is completely independent. With this kind of young adult, maybe parents could help with the down payment on a house.

But if your son always spends more than he makes, and always comes to you with another crisis, and you always give him money, you're what psychiatrists call an enabler. I have what I call a one-time-out rule. If your son gets into trouble because of a history of bad habits, make a deal with him. Tell him you'll get him out of this one fix, but that's it. Next time, he's on his own. If you mean it, and he knows you mean it, it'll stick. If you don't, it will never stop.

One way you can help your child financially without preventing him or her from learning financial responsibility is to be extra-generous—with cash—at birthdays and holidays. If you give your son a nice cash gift for his birthday, you can put some wind in his sails without incurring any ongoing obligation. The amount is up to each family, but a check at Christmas is just fine. That's much better than agreeing to pay half your son's rent.

Many times twenty-something children will ask for their parents' help in buying a car. If this happens, your wisdom and experience should be very helpful, but I strongly recommend that you don't co-sign a car loan. Just as I mentioned with teenagers (in the section on teens and credit), it's a bad idea to put your credit at risk for someone who hasn't learned yet how to pay bills on time. By co-signing, you're not necessarily doing your child any favors anyway. I met a twenty-year-old while I was taping a TV special. The young man had a used truck that was paid for, but he wanted a new one. He was very excited about a truck that cost $38,000. He couldn't qualify for a loan to buy the truck, because he was working only part-time. So his father co-signed a loan for him. The young man's payment on the loan is $650 a month for sixty months. By co-signing, his father ensured that the young man will have almost the equivalent of a house payment to make every month until he's twenty-five years old. And if he doesn't pay, his father gets stuck with it. They both would have been better off if the son bought a vehicle he could afford, or continued to drive the truck he had grown bored with.

If your twenty-something needs money to buy a car, either lend him the money yourself or help him find the best deal on a car loan. One thing that may be available to your twenty-something— and he may not even know how it works—is a credit union. Credit union membership may be available through work, an alma mater, or the community. Credit union loan rates, especially for twenty-somethings, are substantially cheaper than they would be through a car dealership or a bank. Young people, who have not yet established strong credit, may have to pay higher than normal rates. But the maximum rate at a credit union would be lower than the top rates from other lenders. So in that case you're helping your young adult without being on the hook yourself.

If your daughter is a college graduate, she may be able to take advantage of special loans for college graduates. Most of the automakers have them, and the loans are made on favorable terms. In many cases, there are additional discounts or rebates available for people who have recently graduated from college. Carmakers are willing to take that kind of risk because they're betting that the first brand of car you buy may be the car you drive through your lifetime.

Twenty-somethings often don't think about the kind of monthly obligation they're entering into in a car loan. Believe it or not, I've talked with many who have car payments of $600 to $800 a month. They just don't think through how they're going to pay that much each month. Car dealers contribute to that by pitching payments in weekly terms. A $600 monthly payment is $150 a week, and a young person making $500 a week may figure they'll have no problem with that. Of course, adults know that someone making $26,000 a year has no business with a $600 monthly car payment.

Talk to your child about how much of her income should go to a car loan. And help her consider buying a used car, a great value for anyone. You can buy a one- or two-year-old car for as much as 40 percent less than the cost of a brand-new car. That's $15,000 for a used car that would cost $25,000 new.

Give her a few hypothetical examples. If you buy a used car for $10,000 and pay 7 percent interest, what will the payments be over four years? That helps you give your child direction.

What will your payments be?
(Four-year loans at 7 percent)

Car cost	Monthly payments	Total interest	Total payments
$10,000	$239.46	$1,494.20	$11,494.20
$20,000	$478.92	$2,988.39	$22,988.39
$30,000	$718.39	$4,482.59	$34,482.59

One way to make a point with your child is to help her look ahead, or back. If she gets a five-year loan and she's twenty-three, does she really want to be making that payment until she's twenty-eight? If she had gotten that loan at eighteen, she'd just be finishing it at twenty-three. Have her think how long ago that was.

I would much rather a young person get the lesson on what she can afford from a parent. But sometimes you have to let your child learn from the school of hard knocks. Once a young person makes a few $600 car payments and realizes she can't handle it, she'll learn not to do that again the next time.

I talked with a twenty-six-year-old coworker about a continuing problem she had. She had a car she didn't like, so she traded it in after three years. She owed more than the car was worth, so the dealer rolled the balance due into the new car loan. She owned the second car for two years and wanted to get rid of it. It was having some kind of maintenance problem. But she still owed $16,600 on a car that was worth no more than $7,000. She asked me how she could get out of it. A dealer had offered to help her, but he would have taken the $10,000 she still owed, added it to the loan on her next car, and she would be even more "upside down" in that. She didn't like my answer, which was to keep driving it until she paid off the loan. I saw her after our conversation, and she had a new car with dealer plates still on it. So she had decided not to take my advice.

This wasn't my child, of course. It was someone else's child. But the point is that you can give guidance, and most people will hear you and respond, and you'll be able to help prevent trouble. But some won't listen and will have to learn the hard way, and you have to let them.

✳ Moving Back Home ✳

Kids who move back home after college aren't the exception anymore—they're the rule. Two-thirds of all college graduates now move back in with Mom and Dad after they finish school. Most are transitional—they live at home less than one year before getting their first apartment—but a surprisingly large number, 22 percent, still live at home a year after graduating. That's according to a survey by the online job site Monstertrak.

Parents are dealing with children who in some respects are growing up much faster than previous generations, but who are also maturing at a much slower rate. Part of that is they don't fly away from the nest psychologically until about age twenty-five.

Part of the reason for this extended adolescence is financial. If you graduate from college and owe the credit card companies $9,000, you have student loans of $32,000, and you are out looking for your first job, you don't have two nickels to rub together, and you certainly can't afford to pay rent and utilities for an apartment. What are you going to do, live on the street? That's a very logical reason why someone would move back home.

Another part of the reason, I believe, is that houses are so much larger than they used to be, and they have so many more bedrooms than they used to have. That lays out a welcome mat for your kids to move back home. When houses were much smaller 20 or 30 years ago, people were living on top of one another, and the idea of moving back home after college was less appealing for young people.

Of course, a lot of young people don't go to college, or attend college for a while but don't graduate. I get a lot of calls from people who attended two years of college and didn't finish, but still have student loans. They may have a tougher time achieving financial independence.

Another reason some kids are moving back home is to save money to buy a house. I had a caller recently who had just graduated from college and was moving back home for the purpose of being able to save money for a down payment on a house. An intern on my radio show is planning to do the same thing.

Whatever the reason, it can be a tough adjustment for both parent and child when a twenty-something moves back home. Parents have a sense of liberation when their last child leaves the nest and flies off to college. Couples and single parents enjoy the privacy and freedom to do as they please after years of focusing their day-to-day lives on their children. When children move back, that sense of freedom can seem diminished.

Establishing rules is an important step

when a child moves back home. Is the child going to pay rent? Is he going to pay part of the utility bills? Will he buy groceries, or eat your food? Does he have to clean up his room, or can it look like a tornado hit it all the time? Is he expected to clean the house, or clean up a mess he makes if he eats a snack in the living room? These issues are almost like what you would have to deal with if you had a roommate. If a twenty-something wants to live on his own in a pigsty, that's fine. But if he lives in his parents' house, the parent is entitled to set rules. If they don't, parents can feel resentment and anger.

I like the idea of parents charging rent, but if your child is just out of school and has no job and owes everybody, it's probably not realistic to charge rent right off the bat. But as soon as your son or daughter gets a first job, that's when he or she should at least start paying a share of the utility bills and other expenses. If there are three people in the house, have your child pay a third of the electric bill.

There's a great Web site for people who rent property, www.landlord.com. If your child is paying you rent, you are a landlord, so take a look at it.

Having your child back home pre-sents a great opportunity to continue his education about the world of adult finance. Even if you haven't done a great job up until now, this is the chance to immerse him in the things he needs to know to survive financially as an adult. Tell him how much you pay for the mortgage, taxes, natural gas or heating oil, electric, water, cable, and the phone. Tell him how much you earn, and show him a budget, even a rough budget if you don't use one regularly. If he has a job, start working with him on a budget he might use when he gets his first apartment. How much can he afford in rent, for food, for entertainment, after accounting for likely bills? He may think $900 a month to rent an apartment is all he'll need, because he doesn't realize he will have other bills. He'll be a lot more interested in this stuff now than when he was younger, and he may see why he should help offset the extra expenses he creates for you.

I've heard a lot of complaints from parents about outrageous long-distance phone bills after a child moves back. To prevent that, your son or daughter should get a separate phone line, or use a cell phone exclusively. Most cell phone companies provide free long-distance after 7 or 8 P.M., so that's the best way to go. If your twenty-something wants high-speed Internet access, he should pay for that, or at least a share of it.

Food is another very divisive issue. Once you get used to buying groceries for yourself or yourself and your spouse, it's a shock when a ravenous twenty-something moves in. And you hear stuff like "Mom, you didn't get my favorite cereal!" The best solution is separate cabinets and a small refrigerator. Then he can supply his own food. I advised a friend who had a tenant without a separate kitchen or refrigerator. The tenant was using my friend's refrigerator and her food kept disappearing. So I told her to get a second refrigerator—you can buy a small one for about $100—and I haven't heard another complaint about that. If food will be a source of friction, buy your child his own refrigerator and let him buy his own food for it.

Then there's laundry. If your daughter moves back home, it's not your responsibility to do her laundry. Show her how to use the washer and dryer and let her do it herself. Doing laundry for her would raise the resentment quotient in a hurry, because if she were living on her own, there's no way you'd be doing her laundry.

Another thing you have to decide is whether your son or daughter can have a friend spend the night. I got a call from a woman, a single mom, whose daughter had moved back into the house, and her daughter's boyfriend was living with the daughter under the mother's roof. She didn't approve and didn't like the boyfriend. So I told her to kick him out. That idea made her very uncomfortable, but it was her house, and she had a right to decide who lived there and who didn't. You can avoid a big confrontation if you establish house rules on this issue ahead of time.

There can be great benefits in having an adult child move back. Your child can pay some rent and help you with your housing costs, but pay less than she would for her own place. That way, you are helping each other. You might really love your child's company, and enjoy doing things for him or her.

Adult children can also help maintain the house, perhaps mowing the lawn or cleaning the pool. Why would it be realistic to expect twenty-something children to do chores? Because when they have their own homes, they're going to have to do chores, so it makes perfect sense for them to share the load of what needs to be done around your house.

Whether having your child back home works fairly smoothly or not, I like the idea of setting a time limit on your child's stay at your house. If you want her to live there for the long term, great. But if you don't, tell her it's fine to stay for a year after graduation, but after that she needs to find her own place. Remember, you want to help her, but your most important job is to help her achieve true independence.

• Internet •

www.landlord.com *(Tips and information for landlords)*

✳ Your Child's First Apartment ✳

It used to be common in the United States for young couples to live with one set of in-laws for a few years while saving for a house. On TV's *All in the Family*, Archie and Edith Bunker's daughter Gloria and her husband Mike lived with the Bunkers while he finished school. But the afford-ability of housing has made it possible for young people to move out on their own more easily. Rentals represent one third of the housing in this country.

You should advise your twenty-some-thing son about what kinds of things he'll have to deal with when he rents an apart-ment. Often he'll rent with a roommate, and I get calls all the time from people who don't understand what happens when you rent a place with somebody. It's sad to say, but sometimes people get along great until they rent an apartment together. Then, someone doesn't pay his share of the rent, or the phone bill, or the electric bill. Or maybe someone's boyfriend or girlfriend starts sleeping over too often. Or maybe one's a neat freak and the other is a slob.

Everyone who lives in the apartment should be on the lease, but if one doesn't pay, the other is responsible. If one dam-ages the place, the other is responsible. If one skips, the other is responsible. When you sign a lease with someone, you have to make sure you can afford to pay the entire rent in case the other person can't, or won't. I get this call constantly, because roommates don't understand, and their parents don't help them understand, what can happen if things go wrong. It's one of the many school-of-hard-knocks lessons for twenty-somethings.

One way to limit the potential for damage is to sign a six-month lease instead of a one-year lease. That's a good idea even if you have to pay a higher monthly rate. Then, if you hate each other, or someone has to move out, the other roommate might have three or four months to pay on the lease, not eight or nine.

Also, ask the landlord to include a relocation clause that would allow you to terminate the lease, for a fee you would negotiate, if someone has to move out of town. It's not uncommon with twenty-somethings for a first job not to work out, and the roommate might have to relocate for the next job. In most states, you're responsible to pay every month on the lease until the apartment is re-rented. Some leases may include a clause allowing you to terminate the lease in the event of a relocation for two months rent plus the security deposit. That's a lot of money. Negotiate up front and you can probably change that to say if you get a job more than one hundred miles away, the lease terminates and you lose only the security deposit.

As far as utility bills go, the phone is usually the biggest problem area. I recommend you always have long-distance block on a phone that is shared by roommates. Then roommates can use a prepaid calling card or cell phone to make their long-distance calls, and there are no disputes over who owes what. They're a good deal, too. You can buy calling cards now that run just 2.5 cents a minute for calls, and cell phones can often be used to make long-distance calls for free in the evenings.

With electric and gas bills and local phone service, the best idea is for the roommates to split them up. One has the power and gas in his name, the other has the cable TV, water, and local phone. Otherwise, you have to agree over how the bills are to be divided.

✳ Paying off College Loans ✳

As college costs have escalated faster than the rate of inflation, families have relied more on student loans, and that's created a bigger burden in paying them back. I know someone who just finished law school and owes more than $100,000 in student loan debt. Her six-month deferral period is coming to an end, so she'll soon start having to pay back that mountain of debt, and her first job as a lawyer pays $35,000 a year.

The good and bad news about student loans is that you can stretch student loan debt over thirty years, like a mortgage, which lowers the payments and makes them easier to handle. The downside is that you end up paying more money over the life of the loan, which again is just like a mortgage. One of the methods you can choose to repay a student loan is a graduated payment, which lets you pay less at first when your income is lower, then more later as your income grows. As I write this, the interest rates on student loans are the lowest in history. If that continues to be the case, it's a great opportunity for people to lock in the rates of their student loans—what's known as

consolidating them. The rates are so good that if you're twenty-four, I don't care if it takes you until you're fifty-four to pay the loan off.

First, you can't consolidate if you've done it before, unless you have added a new student loan since then. If you are ready to consolidate your loans, check out the Department of Education's loan consolidation site, www.loanconsolidation. ed.gov. They have great rates for consolidating your loans and a useful online guide to doing so. Also shop around with different banks offering consolidations to see if you can get an even better rate.

Despite incredibly low interest rates, a lot of people continue to look a gift horse in the mouth, and don't pay back their student loans. That's a very bad idea, because you can't avoid paying them off. It's important for you as a parent to explain to your child the obligation he has to repay his student loans, and the risks he faces if he doesn't. Student loans for the most part can't even be set aside in bankruptcy.

Until the early 1990s, people didn't take student loans very seriously. They would take out student loans and not pay them back, and the federal government would shrug its shoulders. Then Congress had had enough, and as things do when a pendulum swings, enforcement of student loan payback became vicious. As a result of much tougher enforcement, defaults on student loans dropped to an all-time low of just 5.4 percent at the end of 2003.

Student loan collectors have powers way beyond those of normal bill collectors. As I mentioned in the teens chapter, they can move to deduct loan payments from your paycheck and withhold your tax refunds and have the refund amount applied toward what you owe, plus late fees and collection fees. If you take out student loans, you are going to have to pay them back, no matter what.

I'm not a fan of automatic bank drafts, because there are a lot of problems with accounts being double-debited, or money being taken from you after you have finished an obligation to someone. But with student loans, I recommend that you advise your son or daughter to set up an automatic draft to make the regular student loan payment. That way, the loan gets paid on time every month.

There're three benefits to that. First, it's not as likely that a payment will be missed. As long as there's enough money in the account, the payment will be made. (If there isn't, you could end up defaulting on the loan.) Second, many student loan lenders will give you a break on the interest rate if you pay by draft, and third, many lenders will give you an additional cut in the interest rate, or forgive a portion of your loan, if you make twenty-four consecutive payments on time. Everything is set up to reward you for paying on time.

To make the loan payments, a young person has to have income. Some college graduates may not have jobs in their chosen fields by the time they have to start repaying student loans, but they should be working somewhere. A lot of young people wait tables or work in bookstores until they get their careers rolling, or until they figure out what they want to do. The world is full of underemployed college graduates doing things they wish they weren't doing. As a parent, you're not being cruel or mean if you require your son or daughter to bring in some income. The beauty of that stage of life is not having too much pride, so no job is beneath one. Plus, a twenty-something living at home has no major monthly obligations, so even $250 a week ($6 an hour) is enough to make a difference. The first priority for that income should be paying back those student loans.

* Paying off Credit Cards *

If your twenty-something son moves back home after college and he has credit card debt, that's a great opportunity for him to pay it off. Without the burden of rent or a mortgage, he can throw a big chunk of his income at paying off his credit card debt.

But what I hear a lot from twenty-somethings is they can't figure out how to deal with debt. They continue to use their credit cards, which is a big no-no when trying to cut debt, and their money just disappears, in the mall, restaurants, and nightclubs.

I had a caller recently who moved back home because she had $11,000 in credit card debt, plus her student loans. I told her what you should tell your twenty-something if she's having trouble with credit. First, stop using the cards, because credit cards are an addiction. If you don't pay your balance in full every month, it's an addictive be-

havior, and you have to break that behavior.

Normally, people can't bring themselves to cut up their credit cards, because that's so permanent. So I recommend they put the credit cards in a recloseable freezer bag, fill it with water and put the bag in the freezer. Putting them in a block of ice is a good way to make sure they aren't used. This particular twenty-something didn't like the idea of freezing her credit cards or cutting them up, but she was willing to give them to her mom. I would prefer she not do that, because that helps continue parental dependency. But she was comfortable with this, and I'm for whatever works. This young woman, in her early twenties, was making $45,000 a year, so there was no reason she couldn't pay off that $11,000 quickly. But she was living at home, with few expenses, and her debt wasn't getting any smaller.

This young woman was on a treadmill. She couldn't separate her wants from her needs, and couldn't break her pattern of purchasing. All she really needed from me was an attitude adjustment.

People think of credit cards as a way to get what they want. But credit card debt is a burden that prevents you from spending your money as you wish. Credit card debt makes you weak. If you pay it off, you'll be financially strong again, free to spend, save, or invest as you wish. If you have goals you want to reach, such as buying a car or a house, or going on a nice vacation, credit card debt prevents you from reaching those goals.

This woman, like many young people, had a financial goal—she wanted to buy a house. But she couldn't figure out how to do that because she was in debt and had no money. So I used the goal to help motivate her to get out of debt, and you can do the same with your twenty-something. She wanted to be in a house within eighteen months. So our plan was for her to pay off the $11,000 in credit card debt, plus save enough for a down payment on the house, within that time period. Since she had few expenses—her parents weren't charging her rent—I wanted her to pay off the debt in six months. That meant putting about

$2,000 a month toward the credit card. That would be easy for her, because she was taking home about $2,800 a month. She asked me what she was going to live on, and I said, "You'll live on the difference—$800 a month." Then, she'd spend the next year saving the down payment.

That's the thing I go through with people in their twenties. They're moving back home in huge numbers, and being subsidized by their parents after they've graduated from college. The real challenge is to get them on a solid financial path. You can use what they want, a condo or a house perhaps, to teach them some financial discipline.

If your twenty-something doesn't live at home, and is having trouble handling her finances, the best piece of advice for her is not to buy a fancy car. That's a classic early-twenties error. They'll finish school and go to work, and reward themselves with a new car. But they haven't really bought a car, they've bought an obligation, a monthly payment from a loan or a lease. And that comes back to goals. If your daughter is spending $500 a month on a new car, she can't use that $500 to save for a down payment on a house or condo, or to pay off credit card debt or student loan debt.

Most college students have a car anyway, usually a clunker, maybe a family hand-me-down. So they don't need to buy a new one to get to work. But if the clunker croaks and they need to buy a car, a one- or two-year-old used car is a far better value than an expensive new car. Talk to them before they get new-car fever, and help them avoid lifestyle debts that can divert them from what they really want. The difference between you and your adult child is you've been on your own, probably owned homes, done the things you've wanted to do. So if you choose to spend a lot of money on a car, it won't keep you from achieving the things you've already done. But if a young person buys the new car first, she may not be able to get over that hump.

✳ Kids Who Don't Go to College ✳

Many people don't go to college, and an incredible 73 percent of adults don't have a four-year-college degree.

But many kids who don't go to four-year colleges may go to community colleges, commuter colleges part-time, or trade schools. They're almost always working twenty or so hours a week, so they're stretched between the requirements of work and school.

Ironically, while people who don't get a four-year degree will earn much less over the course of their working lives than will college grads, having to juggle many obligations makes them far more responsible financially in their post–high school years. They mature more quickly than their contemporaries at four-year colleges, who spend their college years in a more sheltered environment.

These young people start earning a real income sooner, so you should start teaching them earlier what to do with that income. It's much better to teach them at eighteen or nineteen, while they're living at home, than when they're twenty-three or twenty-four. Use that period after high school to help your children become less dependent on you. Gradually let them contribute to the household, to the cost of rent, utilities, and food, and get them to start saving for their first house or condo.

Go over your household budget with them and they'll get it much more easily than they did at a younger age, or if they weren't working. They'll be able to see what it costs you to live, and start figuring where they are, or where they need to go.

My daughter Rebecca knows not going to college isn't an option the way I see things. She's going to do what she's going to do, but she will feel massive parental pressure to go to college. And I think, as a parent, you can do your children a tremendous service by educating them about why they should go to college.

While I support community college as a great way to save on the cost of a college education, a lot of the eighteen- to twenty-two-year-olds who don't go to a four-year college may lose the drive to complete their education. They'll go to work more and more and go to class less and less. Then they start missing quarters in school. That really worries me because the value of that four-year-college degree is tremendous in lifting a person's earning power. According to the Employment Policy Foundation, earning a two-year degree will add $229,266 in lifetime earnings, compared to simply completing high school. Earning a four-year degree will increase lifetime earnings by $875,101. Earning a professional-level degree will increase lifetime earnings by $1,609,588. Education is a dependable way to higher earnings.

I remind Rebecca of that continually. She'll see someone doing very hard work, at a job that likely did not require a college education, and I'll remind her that that's why she should go to college. Part of what you should do as a parent is drill into your child how important it is for her, if she wants to live comfortably and be able to support a family, to get a college degree. If she chooses a community college, warn her that it's easier to be diverted away from educational goals by work. For this reason, I recommend that a student attending college should work no more than twenty hours a week. I worked full-time two of the three years of undergraduate school, and then through graduate school, and looking back, I think that was a mistake. It was too much work, working full-time and going to school at night. If they're doing both, encourage your kids not to let work overwhelm education. In the long term, education is so much more important. In the short term, it may look like work is more important.

• **Top Tips for Adult Children** •

○ Your goal should be to help your twenty-something child establish financial independence from you, not to do things that may make him more dependent.

○ Help your twenty-something financially without preventing him from gaining financial independence by being extra-generous—with cash—at birthdays and holidays.

○ Advise your child that when signing an apartment lease with a roommate, he has to make sure he can afford to pay the entire rent in case the other person can't, or won't.

○ If your child doesn't go to college, use the period right after high school to help him become less financially dependent on you. Gradually let him contribute to the cost of running the household and encourage him to start saving.

○ If a child moves back home after college, begin charging him for rent and utilities as soon as he gets a job.

○ Having your child back home presents a great opportunity to continue his education about the world of adult finance.

○ Don't co-sign a car loan for your child. Lend him the money yourself or help him find the best deal on his own car loan.

○ If student loan rates remain at historically low levels, tell your child to lock them in after college, a process known as loan consolidation.

○ Use your twenty-something's financial goals—such as buying a house or a car—to motivate him to pay off his credit card debt.

○ Talk to your adult child before he takes on a $500-a-month car payment, and help him avoid lifestyle debts that can divert him from what he really wants.

CHAPTER 4

Your Parents

Throughout this book, I've talked about how you can teach your children good money values. In this section, we're going to turn the tables.

Now you're the child, and the money relationship is between you and your elderly parents.

✳ Talking with Your Parents About Money ✳

A geriatric social worker told me once that he wants adult children to be "more nosy" about their parents' lives, and that's more true than ever.

People are living a lot longer than they did just a decade ago. There are now more than 4.2 million people age eighty-five or older, according to the 2000 U.S. Census. That's up 37.6 percent from the 1990 Census, which listed 3.08 million people in that age bracket. There were 35 million people age 65 and over in 2000, up 12 percent from 1990. The number of older Americans will continue to grow as the nation ages and health care continues to improve. Members of the giant baby boom generation begin turning sixty-five in 2011.

As our parents age, they may not be as capable of managing their own affairs. We need to poke around more in our parents' financial lives, and help protect them, as they once protected us, from the harsh realities of the world. That kind of role reversal is very difficult, because we don't want to parent our parents, and they often don't want to share information or yield control.

My mother, Joy, is eighty. She's still living independently, even driving a car (although that may not be the best idea). My mother has been taken in by a lot of phony charities, so I've had to stick my nose in her business to help stop that. It's very common for older people to get scammed like this. They're often lonely, and the friendly voice on the other end of the line gets them. I realized after talking to my mother this week that I need to start looking at her credit card statements every month. She called and said there was a charge for $13 on her statement each month and she didn't know what it was for. It was one of those phony savings club memberships that her credit card company helped another firm sell to her. That can happen to people at any age, but it happens much more frequently with

our parents, so we have to protect them against scams.

Most of our parents need help with their end-of-life planning. I'll bet you'd be lucky to find one in fifty people who has had a thorough discussion with her mom or dad about what should happen after they die. Do your parents have a will? Do they have a durable power of attorney for health care that tells you how much medical assistance they want if they're in a coma? If you haven't had these kinds of conversations, and your mom is lying in a hospital bed, what are you going to do? That's why you have to think about this stuff.

My mom and I have reached the stage where she welcomes my involvement in her finances and these various issues. My mom is the kind of person who doesn't want to be bothered with the details, so she takes too little responsibility for them. She enjoys what money buys, but managing money, and setting priorities for how it should be invested, means nothing to her. Persuading her to let me help with that part of her life was relatively easy, because she doesn't treat money as a state secret. She's terribly vulnerable to scams, and she's lucky to have me, and my siblings, to help her say no.

My mom recently got a letter saying that a bond she held had been called. She opened the envelope, saw that it was something about her money, and handed it to me. We'd crossed a key point, and now she's willing to let me help her.

We got there slowly, and that's how I recommend you do it. Don't think you have to have "the talk" with your parents, the one conversation that covers everything. Just like the birds-and-the-bees talk that parents dread when their children are young, the idea of one big talk about finances makes people apprehensive. So do it in small pieces. Ask an open-ended question like "Are you okay financially?" and see what they say. Maybe the answer will be "I'm just barely getting by" or "I'm not paying my bills." That may give you information you need to step in and help.

Try asking your father for some financial advice, because people are always willing to give advice, and in doing so they'll draw from their own experiences. You'll learn a lot about them from what they tell you.

Or ask your parent, "If you die someday (*if* sounds better than *when*), what would you want? Would you want to be buried, or cremated? Do you have a cemetery plot somewhere?" You wouldn't believe how often somebody dies, the next of kin buries them, and it turns out later that they owned a cemetery plot nobody knew about. How would you know if you've never discussed it? People are so uncomfortable with end-of-life discussions that they just avoid the topic entirely.

You should tell your parents what you want, because you could die first, and that's a great way to get into the topic in a nonthreatening way. So your mom might say, "I really want to be buried in the family cemetery plot in Pennsylvania." And your reaction might very well be "I didn't know there was a family cemetery plot in Pennsylvania." Or your mom might have a cemetery plot, but she's changed her mind and now wants to be cremated. Just get those things out on the table. Then, if she doesn't want to be cremated, you can ask what kind of casket she wants. Get as specific as she will let you. You don't want to be a grieving child sitting in a funeral home with some funeral home salesperson who plays the guilt card so beautifully that before you know it, you've spent $10,000 on a casket when your mom wanted a pine box.

It's also important to create a durable power of attorney for health care—a document that gives a family member the power to make decisions for you if you can't, and specifies what you want done. Do you want extraordinary measures taken to keep you alive even if you have no hope of recovery? You, and your parents, can make their wishes clear in this document.

Your parents are more likely to need help when they move from their money-earning to their retirement years. That could be in their sixties or their seventies. The dangers are that they'll outlive their money, or that their health will deteriorate and they won't be prepared to deal with that. Health, finance, and day-to-day living are the key components.

We're seeing the first generation of retirement-age people, sixty-five and seventy, who are helping to care for their parents, who are in their late eighties and nineties and in failing health, even as they are making their own adjustments to retirement. Lifespan elongation creates so many issues.

See where you can have the most impact communicating with your parents about their lives. If they have health problems or have more difficulty living independently, do they want care in the home, or do they want to live in an assisted-living facility?

You're not likely to be completely shut out unless you've had a poor relationship with your parents throughout your life. If that's the case, or if your parents truly don't trust their own children to help with their money, then they should look elsewhere, maybe to a niece or nephew. As a last option, a trust officer at a bank can help people who don't know where else to turn with money management.

Sometimes the problem is which sibling should do what. My father used to tell me that one parent can take care of ten children, but ten children can't take care of one parent. If you're one of many siblings, you probably know which ones are strong or weak in which areas. If you have a sibling who can't follow through, or even get started on problems, he shouldn't be involved. In my family, we have family conferences, in which we discuss who will take on which responsibilities and tasks. My sister does a lot of the medical work. One of my brothers sells group health insurance, so he deals with the insurance side. My other brother and I both deal with the financial side of my mom's life.

Geography can be a big barrier in dealing with an aging parent, with so many families now scattered across the country. My siblings live in three different cities, so we have to overcome that in helping our mother. One of my brothers lives in Macon, Georgia, about ninety minutes from my home in Atlanta, and another brother lives in Arizona. My sister lives in Atlanta. My brother in Arizona comes to Atlanta twice a year on business trips, and he routinely extends his stay by one day so that we can both meet with my mother and go over her finances. Setting up an appointment helps us stay focused.

Another thing you should do, with their approval of course, is have copies of your parents' bank, credit card, and brokerage statements sent to you. Even if the financial institutions charge you a small fee, it's worth it. That makes it easier to watch for red flags, such as excessive credit card spending or a lot of money being given to unfamiliar organizations.

The hard part for me is making the time to give my mom the level of service she needs, and that is an issue many adult children face. With marriage, children, and work, it's hard to find enough time. How do you avoid becoming overwhelmed and set priorities? The biggest thing is getting around to doing the things you say you're going to help your mom or dad with.

Although we can always think of how we could do more, what you do to help your parents makes such a difference in their lives, and it gives you a great opportunity to help pay your parents back for all the wonderful things they did for you growing up and throughout your life.

• Internet •

www.nolo.com	*(Free legal information)*
www.aarp.com	*(Information for you and your parents)*
www.aoa.gov	*(The administration on aging)*
www.nhtsa.dot.gov/people/injury/olddrive	*(Information on older drivers)*

☀ Living with a Parent ☀

If your parents can't live on their own anymore, but you can't afford assisted living, another option is to live together, or at least close to each other.

Having parents live close to you makes it a lot easier to keep an eye on them, to make sure they're eating right and going to the doctor when needed. It's a lot easier to monitor a parent who lives nearby than one who lives in another city. But having Mom or Dad in the spare bedroom might be more than some families can handle. There are a growing number of houses with "in-law suites," which some families use for an older teenager and some for aging parents. They provide a degree of privacy and separation for both parent and child, yet let you keep a close eye on Mom or Dad. It allows you to live separately together, and for many families, that's a great solution. It's certainly a much more affordable solution.

Even if you don't have a house with an in-law suite, it could be worthwhile to create one, using underused space in your house. If it costs $52,000 to live in a nursing home for a year, why not spend $10,000 to modify your home to create semi-independent living quarters in your house for your parents?

Check local zoning codes for possible restrictions on how you can modify your house to accommodate a parent. Some communities will let you include the equivalent of a wet bar with a refrigerator and microwave oven, but they won't let you include a stove, because it's considered a separate residence if it has a full kitchen.

If you can't handle parents living with you, consider having them nearby. My college roommate lives in a suburb of Baltimore, his brother lives in Philadelphia, and his mom lived in New York for many years. He recently moved her into an assisted-care facility in Baltimore because it became too hard to oversee her care as her health deteriorated. By moving her to the same town, he was able to look after her much more effectively.

✳ Long-Term Care Insurance ✳

The cost of nursing home care is so high now, that you could be in a real bind if your parents need to go to a nursing home. The average cost for nursing home care is $52,000 a year nationally, and in some cities it can cost $60,000 to $80,000 per year, according to Metropolitan Life Insurance Co.

Unless you or your parents are wealthy enough to write a check for that amount, you'll have to rely on Medicaid, the federal health program for poor people, to pay for your parents' care. Medicaid won't pay for nursing home care unless the patient is broke, so older people have to spend down their assets to qualify. Widows or widowers have to sell their homes to pay for their medical care before they qualify. A spouse doesn't have to vacate a property for their husband or wife to qualify.

Even then, a lot of nursing homes now don't take Medicaid, so you may not be able to choose a facility that provides a high quality of care if you have to rely on Medicaid. The worst situation is if someone needs nursing home care for a while, then gets better. All the money is gone, and they're out on the street.

A much better option is to buy long-term care insurance, which pays for in-home or nursing home care. If you buy it when you are in your late fifties or early sixties, it's not grossly expensive, and it takes the worry away that a need for long-term care will wreck your finances. The earlier you buy, the better the coverage is and the lower the cost. For example, General Electric's basic long-term policy, for a sixty-year-old in Connecticut, costs $298 a month for a lifetime benefit with inflation protection and an initial daily benefit of $160 per day. By comparison, a seventy-five-year-old in Connecticut pays a premium only moderately higher, $317 per month, but gets vastly inferior coverage. Benefits are for only three years, with no inflation protection, and a daily benefit of only $130.

A few years ago, long-term care insurance policies were so poor, or offered by such questionable companies, that they weren't worth buying. Even today, I've been able to find just eight companies that offer long-term care insurance and are financially sound enough that you can rely on them to provide the benefits they promise. Limit your consideration of long-term care insurance to these eight companies. Four make my honor roll because they're rated A++ for financial strength by A. M. Best: John Hancock Life Insurance Co., State Farm, Mass Mutual, and USAA Life Insurance Co. Four others get honorable mention with A+ ratings from A. M. Best: GE Life and Annuity Insurance Co., Metropolitan Life Insurance Co., Hartford Life Insurance Co., and IDS Life Insurance Co.

In addition to buying a policy from a company that's financially strong, you want a policy that covers both nursing home care and medical care in your own home. There are many situations in which someone needs extra medical attention, but doesn't need to be in a nursing home. Some policies are cheaper because they cover only nursing home care, or limit care to a maximum of two years, but I prefer a policy with a lifetime benefit, or if that's not affordable, five years' coverage. Although some people get better and no longer need nursing home care, most people need more care as they get older, rather than less.

Next, you want a policy that adjusts for inflation, because a benefit that looks reasonable when you or your parents are sixty might seem worthless at age seventy or seventy-five. One insurance industry study projects the cost of nursing home care will rise to $190,600 a year by 2030.

If your parents have moderate wealth, and they're not interested in buying long-term care insurance, then the kids should consider paying the premiums. It's enlightened self-interest. If the parents end up spending down all their wealth, the kids will have to support them. Long-term care insurance protects everyone.

When an aging parent needs enhanced medical attention, it's common for her adult children to move the parent to the city in which they live. Although parents often object, I think it's a good move, because it's just too hard for someone to oversee your care by remote control. If there are several children living around the country, you should consider moving the parent to the city that offers the most affordable nursing home care. New York City is the most expensive city for nursing home care. Shopping around allows you to live within the daily benefit amount provided by the long-term care policy you selected.

Some big companies have an elder

care expert to help you with choices if your parent needs enhanced care, whether it be from a nurse, an assisted-living facility, or a nursing home. If your company doesn't provide that benefit, an elder law attorney can refer you to a geriatric social worker, who can do an evaluation of your parent and advise you what level of care your parent might need. AARP recommends the National Association of Professional Geriatric Care Managers, www.caremanager.org.

• Internet •

www.jhancock.com	*(John Hancock Life Insurance Co.)*
www.statefarm.com	*(State Farm Insurance Co.)*
www.usaa.com	*(USAA Life Insurance Co.)*
www.massmutual.com	*(Mass Mutual Financial Group)*
www.gefn.com/insurance	*(GE Life and Annuity Insurance Co.)*
www.metlife.com	*(Metropolitan Life Insurance Co.)*
www.thehartford.com	*(Hartford Life Insurance Co.)*
http://finance.americanexpress.com	*(IDS Life Insurance Co., now part of American Express)*
www.aarp.org	*(AARP, guide to long-term care insurance)*

✳ Assisted Living ✳

In the continuum of housing and care for the elderly, we think of assisted living as a level between independent living and nursing home care. But assisted living can mean so many different things. It can mean a place that really is providing nursing home–type care without having to meet state standards, or it can mean a gradual increase in the amount of care one receives. It can be any form of housing for senior citizens that is not independent living and not a nursing home—everything in between comes under the assisted-living umbrella.

I have a strong preference for the religious-based, nonprofit assisted-living centers, as opposed to the commercial chains. The Methodists have a fantastic center in

Atlanta, where I live, called Wesley Woods. There's a Jewish-run center that's excellent as well. Both have a campus environment that includes every phase of senior housing, not under one roof but on one campus. As residents need more care, they are shifted from building one to building two, and so on.

Assisted living is a good answer for many seniors who need help but aren't sick enough to be in a nursing home. Twenty years ago, many of these seniors went to nursing homes, but today, nursing homes are for people who are in very poor condition, either because of dementia or physical incapacity. The rest go to assisted-living facilities, receive care from their families, or, if they can afford it, hire in-home health care.

There is no single solution. The health-care industry has struggled with the aging of America, in part because it assumed that the number of people living in institutional settings was going to skyrocket, and it hasn't worked out that way. Nursing homes have such bad reputations, and the idea of putting a parent into a nursing home is abhorrent to some. Yet many families are not able or willing to care for their parents in their homes.

A geriatric social worker can help you figure out what to do—how much intervention to provide for your mom or dad. They can evaluate your parent and recommend a course of care. But the reality is that, if you don't have long-term care insurance, your options as a family are very limited, because the cost of intensive nursing home or in-home care is incredibly high.

If you do have long-term care insurance, there's a good chance your policy will pay a reduced benefit for assisted-living care, compared to nursing home care. You get a percentage of your daily benefit if you live in an assisted-living facility.

With a lot of assisted-living centers, parents pay a large upfront fee, which covers their right to occupy a housing unit. Then they buy the services that they want. As their health deteriorates, they might go from getting one meal a day from the center to getting all their meals provided. It's the same with other services they provide, and it can be a back-door nursing home environment.

Workbook

Activities for
Young Children

Allowance Tracker

Keep track of your allowance! Write the date you get your allowance, what you did to get your allowance (Purpose), and the amount of money (Money Earned/Money Spent). Also write any bonus allowances or extra money you earn. Add your allowance to the total above in the "New Total" column to see how much money you have. If you spend your allowance, write that on the Allowance Tracker, too (Money Earned/Money Spent). *(Make sure you subtract that money, not add it!)*

Date	Purpose	Money Earned/ Money Spent	New Total

Date	Purpose	Money Earned/ Money Spent	New Total

Chore Wheel

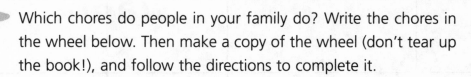

Which chores do people in your family do? Write the chores in the wheel below. Then make a copy of the wheel (don't tear up the book!), and follow the directions to complete it.

Making Your Chore Wheel

You Need:

a pencil or marker

a file folder

construction paper
  or white paper

glue

scissors

a brass fastener

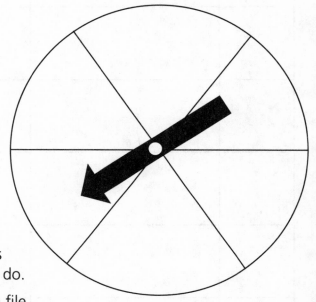

Steps:

1. First, fill in the chore wheel. Write in the chores that people in your family do.

2. Glue the chore wheel to a file folder to make it sturdy.

3. Then cut it out.

4. Draw an arrow on construction paper or white paper, and cut it out.

5. Attach the arrow to the middle of the chore wheel with a brass fastener.

6. Spin the arrow to choose your chores!

Why I Should Get a Bigger Allowance

Do you think your allowance should be bigger? Your parents will want to know why. Fill in this checklist. Check **Yes** or **No** to answer each question. Share the checklist with your family. (If the question doesn't apply to you, then check the last box.)

	Yes	No	Does Not Apply
1. I never forget to do my chores on the chore wheel each week.			
2. I offer to do extra chores without being asked.			
3. I help with my younger brother/sister.			
4. I am a year older than I was when you first decided my allowance.			
5. I am saving up to buy something special.			
6. I need more money to spend with my friends.			
7. I have more responsibilities now at home than when you first decided my allowance.			
8. I'm a good kid and I never get into trouble.			
9. I have shown that I am responsible with my money by saving most of it.			
10. I will continue to be responsible at home, at school, and with my money.			

Thanks!

How Much Can I Buy?

You know how much money you have. But do you know how much you can buy with that money? Do this activity to find out. First, look at each item and how much it costs. Circle the item that costs less.

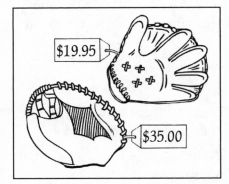

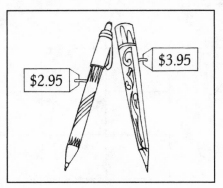

How Much Can I Buy?

You got $50 from your Aunt Edna for a special gift. What can you buy with it? Choose things from page 6 that you'd like to buy with the $50. Add up the prices. If the total is more than $50—whoops! You've spent too much!

Item	Price

Total: _____

Revise your list. Look again at the things that you can buy. Maybe you could choose the same item, but a cheaper one. Maybe you can take something off your list. Remember—you only have $50. Write your new list in the chart below.

Item	Price

Total: _____

Make a Shopping List

Every day, you make choices. You choose which clothes to wear, which shoes to put on, which TV shows to watch, which video games to play. Adults make choices, too. One of the choices they make is about money. Adults must decide what they can buy with the money they have.

One place where they make choices is the grocery store. Help your mom or dad make a grocery list. Write the foods you want to buy. Then write how much you think each of these foods costs. Add up the prices to see how much money you might spend.

Now pretend you can spend $20.

■ Did you buy too much? Cross some things off your shopping list.

■ Did you have money left over? Good for you! You've saved some money.

Now Go Shopping!

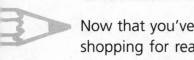

Now that you've had practice with a made-up shopping list, go shopping for real with your family. Follow these instructions to see how your family decides what to buy.

1. First, fill out the shopping list on this page with real things your family needs to buy.

2. Ask how much money your family can spend at the grocery store.

   Write the amount here:
   $_____

3. Now take your list to the grocery store. Take a calculator, too.

4. Write down how much each item costs. Using the calculator, start to add up the prices. Is there enough money to pay for all the things the family wants to buy?

Should some things be taken off the shopping list and bought another time?

Talk about the shopping trip with your family.

Dollars and Cents

When you go shopping, you'll need to give money and get back change. Change comes in dollars and cents. Cents are paid out in coins: 100 cents make up 1 dollar. Add to the coins below to make a dollar. Draw in the coins you need.

1.

2.

3.

4.
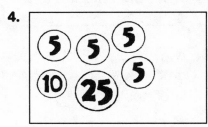

Now look at these items. Pretend you're at the discount store. Which of these things can you buy for $1? Circle or color them.

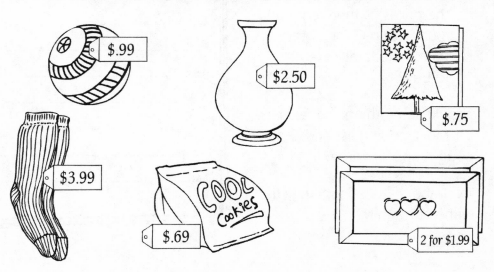

$.99

$2.50

$.75

$3.99

$.69

2 for $1.99

Who Earned More?

Adults and kids do jobs to earn money. Look at the kids below. Each kid did a chore or another simple job to earn some money. Which kid earned more? Add up the money next to each kid, and write the total on the line. Then put a star next to the kid who earned the most money.

1.

$\rule{3cm}{0.4pt}

$\rule{3cm}{0.4pt}

2.

$\rule{3cm}{0.4pt}

$\rule{3cm}{0.4pt}

3.

$\rule{3cm}{0.4pt}

$\rule{3cm}{0.4pt}

Make a Fun Fund

A *fund* is like a piggy bank. It's a place where you keep money to save up for something special. On the line below, write about something special, like going to an amusement park, that you would like to do with your family.

_____

Find a cool place to keep your Fun Fund, like a giant jar or a tin or a shoe box. Decorate your Fun Fund container. Trace the letters below, or make a copy of this page. Then color in the letters any way you want. You can even glue glitter to them or paint them so they glow in the dark! Cut out the letters and glue them to your Fun Fund container.

Now, every time you have change from shopping or money left over from your allowance, put it in your Fun Fund. Ask other people in your family to put money in it, too.

Fun Fund Tracker

Every time you add money to your Fun Fund, write the amount on this Fun Fund Tracker. Keep the tracker near the Fun Fund, too. Tell other people to write what they add to the Fun Fund. Then, when you reach a certain total, take out the money. Then start your Fun Fund again!

Date	Where Did This Money Come From?	How Much Is It?	New Total

Lemonade Stand Plan
PART I

Do you need money for your Fun Fund? Or for something else you want to buy? Some kids make lemonade, and then they sell it. Complete this checklist to get all the things you need. Also write down the cost of the things that you have to buy.

Things We Need for Our Lemonade Stand

___ a table   Where will we get it?_____

___ chairs   Where will we get them? _____

___ pitcher   Where will we get it?_____

___ cups   Where will we get them? _____

___ a sign   Where will we get it?_____

___ money   Where will we get it?_____
box

Things We Need to Make Lemonade

___ lemons   How much do they cost? $ _____

___ sugar   How much does it cost? $ _____

___ water   How much does it cost? $ _____

Lemonade Stand Plan
PART 2

Great! You have everything you need for your lemonade stand. Now think about these questions to complete your plan.

Where?

Where will we set up our stand? _____

Why is this a good **place**? _____

What Day?

What **day** will we set up our stand? _____

Why is this a good **day**? _____

What Time?

What **time** will we set up our stand? _____

Why is this a good **time**? _____

Who?

Who will pour the lemonade? _____

Who will handle the money? _____

Your lemonade stand was a success!

How much money did you make? $ _____
How much money did you spend on supplies? $ _____
Now subtract the bottom from the top number. $ _____

This is your profit! This is how much money your lemonade business made, after spending money on supplies. Good job!

Things We Want—
How Much Do They Cost?

Do you know the cost of the things that you'd like your parents to buy for you? Find out!

1. First, write the things you would like.
2. Then write how much money you think each costs.
3. Now find out how much they cost *for real.* Look in a catalogue or on the Internet. Or go to the store with your family.
4. Draw a star beside the things that cost more money than you thought.

What I Want	How Much I Think It Costs	How Much It Really Costs
1.	$	$
2.	$	$
3.	$	$
4.	$	$
5.	$	$
6.	$	$
7.	$	$
8.	$	$
9.	$	$
10.	$	$

Graph Your Savings!

Now that you know how much something you want *really* costs, try to save the money to buy it. Graph your savings on this bar graph.

1. The first column shows different prices. Find the price for the thing you want. Circle it.

2. The second column has empty bars. Color in the bars up to the price of the item you want.

3. Now count up how much money you have. Find that amount on the graph. Color in the bars of the last column up to this point.

4. Every time you save money, color the bars in the last column to show how much more you have. You can use different colors, if you want.

5. When the bars of the last column reach the bars of the second column, you've saved up all the money you need!

Good job!

$120		
$115		
$110		
$105		
$100		
$95		
$90		
$85		
$80		
$75		
$70		
$65		
$60		
$55		
$50		
$45		
$40		
$35		
$30		
$25		
$20		
$15		
$10		
$5		

Holiday Wish List

The holidays are a time when we give each other presents. You probably would like to get lots of presents. Write your holiday wish list in the first box below.

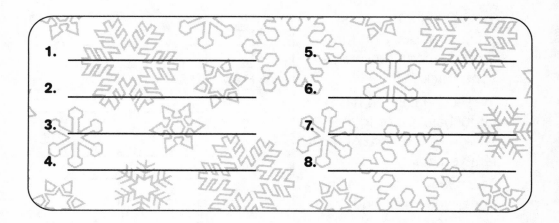

1. _____   5. _____

2. _____   6. _____

3. _____   7. _____

4. _____   8. _____

When you get new things, you might not need all the old things you already have. For each item on your wish list, write something you now have that you could give to someone else. With your family, find a charity that might like your things.

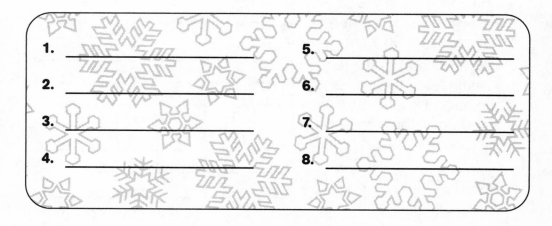

1. _____   5. _____

2. _____   6. _____

3. _____   7. _____

4. _____   8. _____

Clark Smart Parents, Clark Smart Kids

Birthday Wishes

Birthday parties are fun, but they cost money. How much? Find out!

Cost of the Cake

What kind of birthday cake would you like? Go to a bakery or an ice cream store, and find out how much the cake costs to buy. Then find out how much it will cost to make your own cake with your family or with friends.

Cake We Buy	Cake We Make
$	$

Which do you think is more fun—to buy a cake or to make a cake? ☐ Buy ☐ Make

Think about your answers above. What should you do to get a cake? _____

Cost of the Decorations

What kind of birthday decorations would you like? Go to a party store, and find out how much decorations cost to buy. Then find out how much it would cost to make your own decorations with your family or with friends.

Decorations We Buy	Decorations We Make
$	$

Which do you think is more fun—to buy decorations or to make decorations? ☐ Buy ☐ Make

Think about your answers above. What should you do to get decorations? _____

You're Invited!

Like birthday cakes and party decorations, invitations cost money, too. What kind of invitations would you like for your party? Go to a stationery or a party store, and find out. Then find out how much it will cost to make your own invitations with your family or with friends.

Invitations We Buy	Invitations We Make
$	$

Which do you think is more fun—to buy invitations or to make invitations? ☐ Buy ☐ Make

Think about your answers above. What should you do to get party invitations? _____

Let's Get Started!

Here's how to get started making your own invitations. Trace the outline below, or copy this page several times. Or just use it as a guide. Write the information about your party on the lines. Cut out the cards, and fold them in half. On the outside, draw a picture for your invitations. Have fun! And happy birthday!

	You're Invited!
	To: _____
	Where: _____
	When: _____
	What Time: _____
	RSVP: _____
	Hope you can come!

Activities
for Teens

Allowance Tracker

 So maybe you've got a job now, or an allowance, or even several jobs around the neighborhood. Keep track of the money you earn—and the money you spend. Write in the date when you earn or spend your money; then write how you earned it or how you spent it. In the third column, write the amount of money earned or spent. Be sure to add or subtract that amount to arrive at a "New Total."

Date	How Did I Earn It? How Did I Spend It?	Money Earned/ Money Spent	New Total

Chore Wheel

Which chores do people in your family do? How does everyone pitch in and make your home run smoothly? Write the chores and responsibilities in the wheel below. Then make a copy of the wheel (don't tear it out of the book), and follow the directions to complete the chore wheel.

Making Your Chore Wheel

You Need:

a pencil or marker

a file folder

construction paper
  or white paper

glue

scissors

a brass fastener

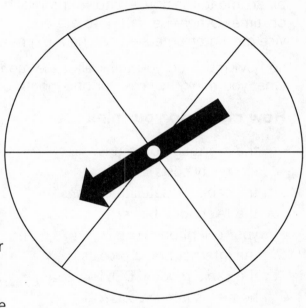

Steps:

1. First, fill in the chore wheel. Write in the chores and other responsibilities that people in your family share.

2. Glue the chore wheel to a file folder to make it sturdy.

3. Then cut it out.

4. Draw an arrow on construction paper or white paper, and cut it out.

5. Attach the arrow to the middle of the chore wheel with a brass fastener.

6. Spin the arrow to choose your chores!

How Much Do You THINK It Costs?

Every month, your parents write checks to "pay the bills." You might even hear them say, "Don't bother me now! I'm paying the bills!" What, exactly, does this mean? Well, every month, your parents have to pay for the things that your family uses every day, like electricity and the telephone and cable TV. Nothing is free. Everything costs money. So every month, bills come to the house, and your family has to make sure the bills get paid on time. Otherwise, late fees are added to the bills, and sometimes service gets interrupted—it can be a big mess!

So how much do you think all these monthly expenses cost? Write down what you think they cost for one month on the lines below.

How much do you think . . .

. . . the mortgage or rent is?　　　　　　　　_____

. . . electricity costs?　　　　　　　　_____

. . . the cable TV/satellite costs?　　　　_____

. . . the telephone bill is?　　　　　　　_____

. . . your cell phone costs?　　　　　　　_____

. . . the Internet hookup costs?　　　　　_____

. . . the cable modem/DSL line costs?　　_____

. . . home insurance costs?　　　　　　　_____

. . . car insurance costs?　　　　　　　　_____

. . . the gas or oil bill is?　　　　　　　_____

. . . the water/sewer bill is?　　　　　　_____

Others: _____　　_____

_____　　_____

_____　　_____

Total monthly expenses:　　　　　　_____

How Much It REALLY Costs

Now ask your parents what these things *really* cost. Ask them to show you some of the bills they get each month. You might also compare the same bill for several months. You'll see that the cost of some items, like electricity and the phone, goes up and down, depending on how much you use them. The bills for other items, like the cable bill and your Internet service, usually stay pretty constant. Compare what you thought these items cost with what they really cost. How close were you?

This is how much . . .

_____	. . . the mortgage or rent is.
_____	. . . electricity costs.
_____	. . . the cable TV/satellite costs.
_____	. . . the telephone bill is.
_____	. . . your cell phone costs.
_____	. . . the Internet hookup costs.
_____	. . . the cable modem/DSL line costs.
_____	. . . home insurance costs.
_____	. . . car insurance costs.
_____	. . . the gas or oil bill is.
_____	. . . the water/sewer bill is.

_____   _____

_____   _____

_____   _____

Total monthly expenses

Mortgage or Rent?

When you looked at the bills your parents pay every month, one bill prob-ably stuck out more than the others. It's a real doozy—the rent bill or the mortgage bill. **Rent** is the money your parents pay to the landlord who owns the apartment building, town house, or other property in which you live. **Mortgage** is the money your parents pay to a bank. Most people don't have all the money needed to buy a house—houses are expensive! In order to buy a house, then, most people go to a bank and get a loan. Every month, your parents pay back some of that loan. That loan is called the mortgage.

Amount Borrowed	Interest Rate	Number of years	Payment per month
150K	7%	30	$997.95
200K	7%	30	$1,330.60
250K	7%	30	$1,663.26
300K	7%	30	$1,995.91
350K	7%	30	$2,328.56
400K	7%	30	$2,661.21
450K	7%	30	$2,993.86
500K	7%	30	$3,326.57

Figuring out how much a mortgage will be is very complicated. It's like a giant math equation! The table on the previous page will give you an idea of how much a mortgage might be.

So Why Not Rent?!

Whew! Figuring out a mortgage is a lot of work. Luckily, real estate agents and bankers know how to do all the little details. And even after all this figuring, the bank still has to approve the buyer. The bank could decide that the person doesn't make enough money or owes too much money to other banks. The bank doesn't believe that the person will be able to pay the mortgage every month. So the bank refuses to make the loan.

Buying a house is a BIG deal and a BIG process!

For many reasons, people often decide to rent a house, a town house, or an apartment. Sometimes rent is cheaper than a monthly mortgage. Sometimes it's not. Do some research, and compare the prices of rentals in your community.

Apartment Complex or Type of Rental   **Monthly Rent**

1.

2.

3.

4.

Now that you know about mortgages and rentals, what do you think? Did your parents make the right decision by buying or renting? What would you do?

Why I Need a Car

Okay, so maybe a mortgage isn't really something that applies to you right now. After all, you have no intentions of buying a house anytime soon. However, there is something you'd really like to buy—a car.

The first thing your parents are going to say when you say you want a car is, "Why?" Next, they'll probably say, "Are you responsible enough to have a car?" Complete this questionnaire to find out. Then you can show your parents the answers to convince them that you should have a car. Circle the answer that best describes you.

1. I have money saved up to help buy a car.

     most   **some**   **not much**

2. I'm working, so I can pay for a monthly car loan and car insurance, as well as gas.

     a lot   **some**   **not much**

3. I'm a responsible driver when I drive your car.

     always   **sometimes**   **not often**

4. I have a job, and I really need a car to get there.

     always   **sometimes**   **not often**

5. I will maintain my car and make sure it's in good working order.

     always   **sometimes**   **not often**

6. I promise never to drive the car anywhere without telling you where I'm going.

     always   **sometimes**   **not often**

7. I promise I won't speed or do anything else illegal in my car.

     always   **sometimes**   **not often**

8. You know you can trust me to be responsible. I view driving as a huge responsibility.

     always   **sometimes**   **not often**

Check Your Score

- If you circled mostly "most" or "always," your parents might agree that you're ready for a car.
- If you circled mostly "some" or "sometimes," you might have to make some changes before your parents will agree with you. Talk over these points with your parents, and discuss what you can do to change their minds.
- If you circled mostly "not much" or "never"—well, maybe you're not quite ready for a car yet. Reevaluate your position in a few months; then try this questionnaire again.
- Your parents will want to hear *why* you should get a car, not just, "Because I want one."

Car Budget Worksheet

Yay! Your parents have agreed to let you buy a car. Now you have to do some figuring. Like everything else, cars cost money. You need to set a car budget. Just as your parents pay the monthly bills, you will have to pay monthly bills for your car, too, like a car payment, an insurance payment, gas, even repairs. Figure out how much you're willing to spend each month. This will help you realize what kind of car to buy. Complete the chart with money amounts you discover when you complete pages 138 and 139.

1.	How much money do you have to spend on a car every month?	
2.	What is the most you can pay for a car loan each month?	
3.	What is the most you can pay for car insurance each month?	
4.	What is the most you can pay for gas each month?	
5.	You never know when your car might break down. You should try to put money in savings in case this happens. Car repairs can be expensive! How much are you willing to save for future car repairs?	
Add the amounts in Boxes 2 through 5:		
Look at Box 1. Do you have enough money each month for a car?		

How a Car Loan Works

 A car loan is similar to a mortgage, but with a lot less figuring and fees. The amount of the loan each month depends on these things:

1) the price of the car

2) the amount of money you put down

3) the amount of interest the bank charges for the loan

4) the number of months you take to pay off your loan

You might have a special car in mind, but can you afford to buy it? Find out.

Write the car you would like on the line below.

_____

Now find out how much that car costs, and see the table below for an idea of whether you can afford the monthly car-loan payment. Then you can use the table again to figure out loan payments for other cars.

Amount Borrowed	Interest Rate	Number of years	Monthly Payment	Total Interest Paid
20,000	5%	3	599.42	1,579.05
20,000	5%	4	460.59	2,108.12
20,000	5%	5	377.42	2,645.48
20,000	5%	6	322.10	3,191.10
20,000	5%	7	282.68	3,744.97

What's Up with Insurance?

Insurance is something that every car owner—and driver—must have. Insurance isn't something you see or hold in your hands. Insurance is a kind of protection that keeps you and your money safe if you have an accident or something else bad happens to you when you are driving.

Basically, you pay money to an insurance company for your insurance. Then, if you get in an accident, the insurance company will pay to fix your car. If the accident was your fault, the insurance company will also pay to fix the other person's car. If the accident wasn't your fault, then usually the person who caused the accident will have their insurance company pay you. Car repairs caused by an accident can be very expensive. So can hospital bills. When you have insurance, you insure that all these things will be paid.

Most likely, your parents added you to their car insurance policy when you started to drive. So you have insurance through them. Ask your parents how much they pay for a teen driver, and write the amount below. Then do some research. Go on the Internet, or call some other car insurance companies. See how much they charge to insure a teen driver. You might also check out how much they charge to insure other drivers. You may be surprised! Insurance companies think you're a risk! They think you are more likely to get in an accident than older people. So your insurance rate is probably higher than your parents'!

Insurance Company	Rate for Teen Driver	Rate for Older Driver

Car Quest

Check it out! Just as car insurance companies charge more to insure teen drivers, they also charge more to insure expensive cars. For example, fixing damage on a new car costs more than fixing damage on an old car, so new cars usually cost more to insure than older cars. Also, some cars are considered more valuable than others (that is, they cost more in general), so the insurance companies charge higher rates for those cars. The insurance for, say, a brand-new Hummer probably costs a lot more than the insurance on a used Corolla.

Before you decide on a car, then, you need to see how much the insurance company will charge you for that car. Choose an insurance company you've felt comfortable with so far in your research. It might even be the one your parents have. Then see how much it charges for different cars. Color in the bars below to help you see the difference.

Car:_____

Insurance per year:

$100	$200	$300	$400	$500	$600	$700	$800	$900	$1000+

Car:_____

Insurance per year:

$100	$200	$300	$400	$500	$600	$700	$800	$900	$1000+

Car:_____

Insurance per year:

$100	$200	$300	$400	$500	$600	$700	$800	$900	$1000+

What Is
Credit and Debit to You?

These days, people more and more often buy things with credit cards or debit cards, rather than with cash. But what do these cards really mean? How is handing over a credit or a debit card "paying" for something? Answer the questions below. Write what you think credit cards and debit cards are all about.

What—to you—is a CREDIT card? _____

_____

_____

Why should you have one? _____

_____

_____

What—to you—is a DEBIT card? _____

_____

_____

Why should you have one? _____

_____

_____

Now share your answers with your parents.

Credit Card Quiz

Think you know all there is to know about credit cards? Take this simple quiz to find out. Circle true or false for each statement. Then turn the page to check your answers.

1. Using a credit card is just like having free money.   **true**   **false**

2. I can buy anything if I have a credit card, no matter how much it costs.   **true**   **false**

3. Credit cards are great because if I don't have the money, I can still buy what I want.   **true**   **false**

4. Using credit cards is a great way to establish credit.   **true**   **false**

5. Every month, the credit card company sends me a bill.   **true**   **false**

6. The bill shows me where I used my card and how much money I spent there.   **true**   **false**

7. The minimum amount due is the least amount of money that I can pay each month.   **true**   **false**

8. The due date is the day I need to mail my payment.   **true**   **false**

9. If I don't pay the bill on time, the credit card company charges me a late fee.   **true**   **false**

10. The interest rate is the rate of interest that I show by using one credit card instead of another.   **true**   **false**

11. If I don't pay off the full balance due, the balance due stays the same.   **true**   **false**

12. Paying the minimum amount due on time means I will pay off my credit card really fast.   **true**   **false**

13. The most responsible way to pay off a credit card is all at once.   **true**   **false**

14. I should *not* pay off my credit card all at once. After all, why use a credit card if I have the money?   **true**   **false**

15. It is really difficult to get into financial trouble by using credit cards.   **true**   **false**

Credit Card Quiz

Check Your Answers

Now see if you understand all about credit cards. Read the answers shown here, and compare them with your own.

1. **False.** It might *seem* like a credit card is free money, but that couldn't be further from the truth. When you pay with money, you have totally bought the item. You never have to worry about paying for it again. When you pay with a credit card, you've only put off paying until sometime in the future. Eventually, you'll have to "really" pay for it.

2. **False.** Credit cards have limits, and you can't spend more than that limit. For example, if the limit is $500, and you want to buy a computer for $1,000, the credit card company won't let you spend more than the $500 limit.

3. **True, sort of.** Sure, you can buy what you want if you don't have the money—now. But you will need to have the money eventually to pay the bill. So don't go crazy!

4. **True, sort of.** Yes, credit cards will help you establish credit, but they can also help you establish *bad* credit. If you pay bills late or not at all, you show that you're not responsible with your money. This makes you a credit *risk.* So in order to establish good credit, you have to use credit cards wisely and responsibly.

5. **True.** Yes, every month, the credit card company will send you a bill.

6. **True.** Your credit card statement lists all your purchases. It doesn't state exactly what you bought, but it does show where and when you bought it and how much it cost. It's a good idea to keep your credit card receipts, so you can match them against the bill to make sure there hasn't been a mistake.

7. **True.** Most credit cards ask you to pay not the entire amount, but only part of it. However, paying the minimum is sometimes not the best idea. See #12.

8. **False.** The due date is the day that your payment needs to be at the credit card office. If you mail your payment on the due date, the credit card company will get your payment late. A good rule is to mail your payment a week before it is due, at least. Better yet, pay your bill as soon as you get it!

9. **True.** Late fees can be anywhere from $10 to $50! Just because you missed the payment date! AND these late payments go against your good credit. Always try to pay your bills on time. You'll save money and avoid hassles later on.

10. **False.** The interest rate is the percentage that the credit card company charges you for your purchases. Some interest rates are low, like 8 percent. Others are very high,

like 20 percent. The interest rate is stated on your bill. It's probably called "annual interest rate." That means that over one year, the credit card company charges you that percentage of interest on the average amount of money you spend. So if you buy $1,000 worth of stuff and you carry that balance for the whole year, the credit card company might charge you as much as $200 that year for your purchases. That's how the credit card company makes money—by charging you interest.

11. **False.** If you buy something for $200 and you send the credit card company $50, you might think your next bill will be $150, right? Wrong! Remember—the credit card company charges you interest on how much money you owe. So your new bill will be $150 plus the interest.

12. **False.** Paying the minimum amount due might seem like a great deal. You buy lots of stuff and pay only a fraction each month. But the longer it takes to pay off the credit card, the more interest you pay also. Remember, interest is the amount the credit card company charges you for making your purchases. Every month, the credit card company adds interest charges to your bill. So if you pay $50, but your interest charge is $45, your credit card bill is only going down by $5! Pay off as much of the bill as you can.

13. **True.** The best way to prevent extra interest fees is to pay off your credit card balance all at once. Period.

14. **False.** People use credit cards for a variety of reasons. Sometimes people don't like carrying cash, so they'd rather use credit cards. Some items, like computers, cost much more money than people usually carry with them. Credit cards are convenient, but they must be paid off. Period.

15. **False.** It is *very easy* to get into trouble with credit cards. Credit cards seem like free money. But if you can't pay the credit card bills, the credit card companies will send you letters and call you and bother you and eventually send your bill to a collection agency—a company that collects bad debts. That's serious stuff! And it can hurt you later, when you're older and you want to buy a car or a house.

Check Your Score!

11–15 right: You're a credit card guru. You understand the pros and cons about using credit cards. You might be ready for one of your own.

6–10 right: You're a credit card wannabe. You need to understand a little bit more about when to use credit cards and how to be responsible with them. You're probably not yet ready for a credit card of your own.

1–5 right: Uh-oh! You're a credit card nightmare! You don't understand at all the consequences of using credit cards. If you had a credit card now, you could get into serious trouble. Try to find out more before you use them.

Your Credit Card Personality

It's really tempting to use credit cards. Do you think you'd always use them wisely? Read the scenarios below. Circle the answer that best tells what you would do.

1. Your parents give you a credit card to buy new stuff for school. They tell you not to spend more than $200. You . . .
   a) buy whatever you want—after all, credit cards don't have limits. How will they know how much you spent?
   b) buy a few extra things, and tell your parents you'll pay them back.
   c) pick a few things and make sure the price doesn't go over $200.
   d) buy some extra things with your friend's credit card.

2. Your parents give you a credit card for emergencies. You're at the mall, and you see the coolest new gadget—you just have to have it. You . . .
   a) whip out the credit card. Your parents will understand this "emergency."
   b) call your parents and ask if they'd mind if you used the credit card.
   c) think of ways you could save money, and buy the item in the future.
   d) use the credit card, and then hope your parents don't notice it on the bill.

3. Your parents have agreed to give you a credit card. You . . .
   a) take all your friends on a huge shopping spree.
   b) treat all your friends to dinner at a trendy restaurant.
   c) leave the credit card in your room so you won't use it foolishly.
   d) put the credit card in your wallet so you can use it whenever you want to.

4. Even though you have a job, you run out of money to go with your friends to the movies. You know that some movie theaters now take credit cards. You . . .

a) go to the movies and use your credit card to buy tickets for you and all your friends.

b) go to the movies and use your credit card to buy yourself a ticket.

c) choose not to go to the movies because you have no money.

d) use your credit card to get a cash advance, then go to the movies.

5. You've paid for your senior trip or for the prom with your credit card, and now you're totally maxed out. You want to use your credit card on the trip or at the prom. You . . .

a) call the credit card company and ask them to increase your limit.

b) ask your parents for another credit card.

c) pay off your credit card as quickly as possible.

d) pay the minimum balance each month until the trip.

6. You want to buy your boyfriend or girlfriend a really great gift, but it costs way too much money. You . . .

a) put it on your credit card, even though you won't be able to buy anything else.

b) pay half with cash, and half with your credit card.

c) buy something cheaper so you don't run up your credit card.

d) take out a cash advance against your credit card and buy the gift with cash.

Check Your Score!

If you answered mostly A's—Hold on! You need to curb your credit card habits. You like to live for the moment and pay the consequences later. You'll pay, all right—and pay and pay and pay. Learn some restraint!

If you answered mostly B's—Almost! You show some restraint when it comes to using credit cards, but you could still get in trouble. Be careful!

If you answered mostly C's—Excellent! You understand that credit cards are not free money. You are a responsible credit card holder.

If you answered mostly D's—Not yet! You don't really get what it means to use a credit card. You need to learn more about the responsibilities and consequences of having a credit card.

"Check" It Out!

So now you have a credit card bill to pay, maybe even a car loan, and a job, too. How should you handle your money? By keeping it in a checking account. Checking accounts allow you to make deposits—put money in the bank—and write checks to pay bills. You might already know about checking accounts, but here's a refresher course, just in case.

Sample Check

Your name and address appear on your checks. You can have your phone number printed here, but you should never have your Social Security number printed on your checks. Then anyone can see it and might "steal" it. (This is what often happens during "identity theft.") *

On this line, write the date you write the check.

Every check has a check number. The numbers help you keep track of your checks. You write the numbers in your checkbook register.

On this line, write the name of the person or company that gets the money.

In this box, fill in the amount of the check.

On this line, spell out the amount of money that you wrote in the box.

This line is for your signature. Checks aren't valid unless they are signed.

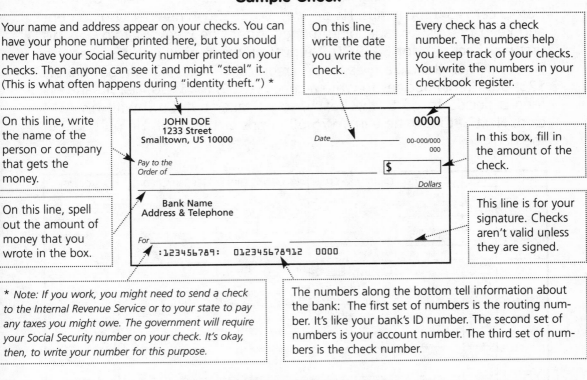

JOHN DOE
1233 Street
Smalltown, US 10000

0000

Date_____ 00-000/000
000

Pay to the
Order of _____ $

Dollars

Bank Name
Address & Telephone

For_____ :123456789: 012345678912 0000

* Note: If you work, you might need to send a check to the Internal Revenue Service or to your state to pay any taxes you might owe. The government will require your Social Security number on your check. It's okay, then, to write your number for this purpose.

The numbers along the bottom tell information about the bank: The first set of numbers is the routing number. It's like your bank's ID number. The second set of numbers is your account number. The third set of numbers is the check number.

Sample Checkbook Register

Write the check number here.

Write the date you write the check here.

Write why you wrote the check here. (Who is the check for?)

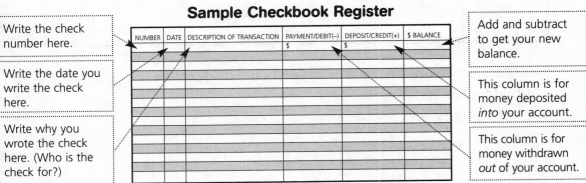

NUMBER	DATE	DESCRIPTION OF TRANSACTION	PAYMENT/DEBIT(–)	DEPOSIT/CREDIT(+)	$ BALANCE
			$	$	

Add and subtract to get your new balance.

This column is for money deposited *into* your account.

This column is for money withdrawn *out* of your account.

Now Try It

Now that you know what the columns on a check register mean, try keeping track of the money for the kid in the paragraph below. Start by writing the money he initially has. Then follow the story to complete the check register.

Harold has a summer job waiting tables at the local diner. His checking account starts with a balance of $151.36. After his first night of work, Harold earns $46.50 in tips. He decides to put $20 in his checking account and keep the rest for spending money. After one week, Harold gets his first paycheck. It's for $479.20. He puts all this money into his checking account. Then the bill arrives for his credit card. The minimum payment is $25, but Harold decides to write a check (#235) for $100. Harold and his friends decide to go to the beach, so he takes out $100 with his ATM card. Next Saturday, he earns $75.60 in tips at the diner. He puts $50 in the bank.

NUMBER	DATE	DESCRIPTION OF TRANSACTION	PAYMENT/DEBIT(–) $	DEPOSIT/CREDIT(+) $	$ BALANCE

The last balance on the check register should be $500.56.
- If that's what you got, good for you!
- If not, go back and see where you messed up.

The Cost of College

You might be starting to think about where you'd like to go to college. Just like everything else, colleges and universities cost money. *Tuition* is the money you pay to attend the school and take classes. *Room and board* is the money you pay to live on campus and eat in the dining hall. If you go to a college near where you live, you might live at home, so you don't have to pay room and board. If you decide to go away to school, you'll probably have to pay these fees.

How much do room and board and tuition cost? Find out! Research the schools you'd like to go to. Then share these costs with your parents.

School	Cost of Tuition	+	Cost of Room and Board	=	Total for One Semester
		+		=	
		+		=	
		+		=	
		+		=	
		+		=	
		+		=	
		+		=	
		+		=	
		+		=	
		+		=	
		+		=	
		+		=	

Choosing and Paying for College

Have an honest discussion with your parents about how you can all work together to pay for college. Your parents may have a special savings account, called a college fund, set aside for you already. But they might not. Use this work sheet to help you and your parents decide if the school you want to go to is "do-able."

College I would like to go to: _____

I want to go here because: _____
_____
_____

Tuition per semester: _____   Tuition per year: _____

How We Can Pay for College

Money in a college fund or savings account: _____
Parents' contribution: _____
My contribution: _____
Any scholarships: _____
Any federal or state assistance: _____
Can we get a student loan?   _____
How much will the student loan cover?   _____

In Conclusion . . .

Is it realistic for me to go to this school? Explain your answer.

_____
_____

Should You Really Get a Job?

You can probably think of a million reasons why you need a job—and just as many reasons why maybe you don't. Jobs are great for earning and saving money. But jobs can also take up a lot of time. Take this quiz to help you decide if you should get a job. Circle the answer that best describes you and your situation.

1. You have time after school and on the weekend to devote to a job.

mostly true   **somewhat true**   **not really true**   **totally false**

2. Your grades are pretty good, and they won't suffer if you have a job.

mostly true   **somewhat true**   **not really true**   **totally false**

3. You have a car or another way to get to work.

mostly true   **somewhat true**   **not really true**   **totally false**

4. You're trying to save money for college.

mostly true   **somewhat true**   **not really true**   **totally false**

5. You're trying to earn money so you don't have to borrow from your parents.

mostly true   **somewhat true**   **not really true**   **totally false**

6. You don't have lots of after-school activities planned.

mostly true   **somewhat true**   **not really true**   **totally false**

7. You won't be breaking other commitments at home (like taking care of a young brother or sister) or at school (like a school club or team) by taking this job.

mostly true   **somewhat true**   **not really true**   **totally false**

8. The hours are okay and won't interfere with your schoolwork or homework.

mostly true   **somewhat true**   **not really true**   **totally false**

9. You feel that having a job will give you a new perspective on earning money.

mostly true   **somewhat true**   **not really true**   **totally false**

10. You feel that having a job will give you a new perspective on the value of money.

mostly true   **somewhat true**   **not really true**   **totally false**

11. You are responsible enough to stick to a work schedule and show up on time.

mostly true   **somewhat true**   **not really true**   **totally false**

12. You will be responsible with the money you earn from your job.

mostly true   **somewhat true**   **not really true**   **totally false**

13. You plan on putting some of the money you earn in a savings or checking account.

mostly true   **somewhat true**   **not really true**   **totally false**

14. You want to learn real-world skills that might help you when you're older.

mostly true   **somewhat true**   **not really true**   **totally false**

Check Your Score!

• **If you answered mostly MOSTLY TRUE: You're hired!** You seem to have a good idea of what it means to have a job, and your schoolwork and other commitments won't suffer because of it. Getting a job is probably the right thing for you.

• **If you answered mostly SOMEWHAT TRUE: Give it a try!** Having a job is probably a good idea, but you might need a bit of help keeping on track with school, your finances, and other obligations. Give the job a trial run and see how it goes.

• **If you answered mostly NOT REALLY TRUE: Uh-oh!** You're probably not ready to have a job. Your reasons for wanting a job are misguided, and you might spend your money—and time—unwisely. You need an attitude change before you're ready to join the workforce. Try again in a few months.

• **If you answered mostly TOTALLY FALSE: Time to Punch Out!** If you were to take a job at this point, your schoolwork might suffer, and you wouldn't be responsible with your work schedule or your income. It's probably better to focus your energies on doing well in school and helping out at home.

Paying Attention to Your Paycheck

Congratulations! You've landed a great job. It fits in with your school schedule, you have no problem getting to work, and, so far, you like what you do. You can't wait to get your first paycheck. It should be at least—hey! What are all these deductions?!

Your paycheck reflects not only your wages and the hours you work, but also money taken out by the government. Every person who works has to pay taxes to the federal government and the state government. Money is also deducted from your paycheck for Social Security and sometimes for insurance. To better understand the notations on your paycheck, complete this work sheet.

What It Says	What It Means	What Are Your Numbers?
Rate	The rate is how much money you make per hour.	
Hours	The hours are the amount of time you worked during that pay period.	
Earnings	Your earnings are how much money you made. (Multiply your rate by your hours.)	
Ded. or **Deductions**	This is money that has been taken out of your check.	
Fed. or Federal	This is the federal income tax.	
St. or State	This is your state income tax.	
FICA	FICA is your contribution to Social Security.	
DI	DI means "disability insurance," which some states collect.	
Other?	Write about it here, then ask your folks.	

The Week Ahead

So you have a job. And school. And homework. And after-school activities. And stuff to do at home. Do you have time for all these things? One way to make sure you do is to create a schedule and try to stick to it. Fill in the schedule below. Be sure to note the times when you need to do things, too. If any times overlap, then you have a scheduling conflict. (You might make copies of this schedule to use again.)

Day of the Week	After-School Activities	Job (Work) Schedule	Homework	Commitments at Home	Time for Fun
Sunday					
Monday					
Tuesday					
Wednesday					
Thursday					
Friday					
Saturday					

Saving Up

When you start earning money, you can start saving for things you want to buy. The best way to start saving is to first find out how much something costs (your goal). Then you need to figure out how much money you can save each week toward that goal. Divide the total cost by your savings each week, and you'll find out how soon the purchase can be yours. (Hint! The more you save each week, the sooner you buy it.) Research some things you really want, and then fill in the coupon boxes below to figure out a savings plan.

What I Would Like to Buy: _____

How Much It Costs: _____

How Much I Can Save Each Week: _____

How Many Weeks I Will Need to Save Up: _____

If I start saving_____, I can buy it_____.

What I Would Like to Buy: _____

How Much It Costs: _____

How Much I Can Save Each Week: _____

How Many Weeks I Will Need to Save Up: _____

If I start saving_____, I can buy it_____.

What I Would Like to Buy: _____

How Much It Costs: _____

How Much I Can Save Each Week: _____

How Many Weeks I Will Need to Save Up: _____

If I start saving_____, I can buy it_____.

Are You a Saver or a Spender?

Do you think you're more of a saver or a spender? Take this short personality quiz to find out. Circle the answer that best describes what you would do in each situation.

1. Your grandparents give you $100 for your birthday. You . . .

a) put it in your savings account.

b) treat your friends to the movies and popcorn.

c) buy a cool pair of shoes you've been eyeing.

2. Your boss gives you a raise. You . . .

a) add more money each week to your savings plan.

b) celebrate by taking your family out for pizza.

c) get excited because you have more money to spend each week.

3. You win a contest at work and get a $50 cash prize. You . . .

a) put some in your checking account—you have a really big credit card bill to pay.

b) buy ice cream for your coworkers—they helped you win the prize.

c) buy some new CDs.

4. You find an extra $20 when doing the family laundry. You . . .

a) add the money to your savings account—you're that much closer to getting something great!

b) give the money to your parents—it could be theirs.

c) go to the mall to see how you can spend it.

Check Your Score!

• **If you answered mostly A's—You're a Saver! Good for you!** You value your money, and you like to see your savings accumulate and grow. You'll soon be able to buy that something big or special you've always wanted.

• **If you answered mostly B's—You're a Generous Spender!** You like to spread your money around so others can enjoy it. This is very admirable and very generous of you. But don't forget to take care of yourself, too!

• **If you answered mostly C's—You're a Spender!** You go for instant gratification and buying something now, rather than waiting and saving to get something bigger and better. Spending is okay—as long as you're not missing out.

Let the Savings Begin! But Where?

Banks offer several ways for you to save your money. Do you know the difference? Do some research about checking accounts, savings accounts, and Roth IRAs. Write what you discover in the chart below. (You can ask your parents, visit a bank, or check out a bank online.) Then discuss with your parents which type of account might be best for you.

	Checking Account	Savings Account	Roth IRA
What is the primary purpose of this account?			
Does this account yield any interest?			
If so, what is the interest rate?			
How accessible is my money?			
What fees do I have to pay?			
Is a minimum balance needed?			
If so, what is the minimum balance?			
Conclusion:			

Savings Tracker

You should think about your savings plan like a fund drive—a fund drive that collects money for YOU! Use the outline below to track how much money you save. Choose a color for your contributions, any contributions your parents make, and any contributions you get from other sources (like other family members). Color in your fund drive until you've reached your goal. To get started, write the money increments on the lines (like $20, $40, $60; or $50, $100, $150, etc.). The lowest should be at the bottom.

How much did you and your parents each contribute? Color in these bar graphs to compare your contributions

[Ex: $40]

[Ex: $20]

$0

You

Your Parents

Other

Your Dream Job

The job you have now is probably not what you'll be doing when you are older. What job would you like to have then? Why? Give it some thought, then list your dream jobs, in order from most to least interesting. Explain why you'd like each job, too.

My Dream Job	Why I'd Like This Job
1. _____	_____
	_____
	_____
2. _____	_____
	_____
	_____
3. _____	_____
	_____
	_____
4. _____	_____
	_____
	_____
5. _____	_____
	_____
	_____

Is the Job
Really a "Dream"?

When you choose a dream job, you have ideas and expectations about it. But are your ideas realistic? Do some research to find out. List your dream jobs on the chart. Then find out the education or training you need, what the job really entails, and the average salary.

Dream Job	Education or Training	A Day on the Job	Average Salary
1.			
2.			
3.			
4.			
5.			

Has learning more about your dream jobs changed your ideas? Write any new ideas you have about your dream jobs on the lines below.

1. _____

2. _____

3. _____

4. _____

5. _____

Comparison Shopping

One way to save money is to cut back on how much money you spend. That doesn't always mean you have to buy less. Sometimes it just means you have to buy things that cost less. Do some comparison shopping. In the first column below, write about things you like to buy, like clothes, shoes, jewelry, movie tickets, CDs. Then see if you can find a place that sells something similar, but for less money.

Things I Like to Buy	Comparison Shopping	Difference
What is it? _____ Where do I usually buy it? _____ How much does it cost? _____	What is it? _____ Where did I buy it this time? _____ How much does it cost? _____	This is how much money I can save! _____
What is it? _____ Where do I usually buy it? _____ How much does it cost? _____	What is it? _____ Where did I buy it this time? _____ How much does it cost? _____	This is how much money I can save! _____
What is it? _____ Where do I usually buy it? _____ How much does it cost? _____	What is it? _____ Where did I buy it this time? _____ How much does it cost? _____	This is how much money I can save! _____
What is it? _____ Where do I usually buy it? _____ How much does it cost? _____	What is it? _____ Where did I buy it this time? _____ How much does it cost? _____	This is how much money I can save! _____

Sales Pitch

 Another way to save money is to buy things when they go on sale. Clothing stores, department stores, music stores, all-purpose stores—they all have sales, sometimes every week. The best place to search for sales is in the Sunday newspaper, which is loaded with flyers and advertisements for sales. Take a look at the flyers in your Sunday paper. Jot down below things that you'd like to buy and how much they cost on sale. Then write down how much the item usually costs. (The flyer often lists the regular price.) Note how much money you can save!

Store Name	Item	Sale Price	Regular Price	Savings

Prom Planning

Do you know exactly how much money you'll need for the prom? Complete this work sheet to find out. Each expense has three columns to fill in, so you can do some comparison shopping. Note different places to buy each item, as well as the different prices. Then you can see where you might want to save money or spend a bit more.

Don't forget the cost of the prom itself! How much is your school charging you for the prom? $_____

Prom Expense	Price 1	Price 2	Price 3
Dress/Tuxedo	Store: _____ Outfit: _____ How much? $ _____	Store: _____ Outfit: _____ How much? $ _____	Store: _____ Outfit: _____ How much? $ _____
Corsage/ Boutonniere	Store: _____ Arrangement: _____ How much? $ _____	Store: _____ Arrangement: _____ How much? $ _____	Store: _____ Arrangement: _____ How much? $ _____
Limo	Company: _____ Type of Vehicle: _____ How much? $ _____	Company: _____ Type of Vehicle: _____ How much? $ _____	Company: _____ Type of Vehicle: _____ How much? $ _____

Prom Savings

One price for the prom remains constant: the price your school charges you to go to the prom. You can't skip on this payment or find a cheaper price! But you might be able to save money on the other expenses. If saving on the prom is an issue, try to come up with ways you can enjoy the prom without spending as much money. Think over ideas with your friends or even with your parents. Write your ideas below.

How much does the prom cost?   **$**_____

This is a cost I *can't* change. But maybe I could . . .

. . . save money on dinner? Here's how:

_____

_____

_____

. . . save money on a limo? Here's how:

_____

_____

_____

. . . save money on flowers? Here's how:

_____

_____

_____

. . . save money on a dress/tuxedo? Here's how:

_____

_____

_____

One-Stock Shopping

You've probably heard about the stock market, right? But what is it, exactly? Well, very simply, stocks are small pieces of a company that you own. Most major companies sell stocks, and the people who buy the stocks become "stockholders." When a stock price goes up, the value of the stock increases. Of course, when the stock price goes down, the value of the stock decreases. So buying stocks can be a gamble.

Think about companies that you might like to own a piece of, like a computer company, a restaurant, a store, even a website. Write the companies below, and explain why you'd like to own stock in each one.

Company: _____

What does this company do? _____

Why I'd like to own some of this company's stock: _____

_____

_____

Company: _____

What does this company do? _____

Why I'd like to own some of this company's stock: _____

_____

_____

Company: _____

What does this company do? _____

Why I'd like to own some of this company's stock: _____

_____

_____

Stock Tracker

Now pretend to buy some stock, and see how you do. First, choose one of the stocks you wrote about on page 165. Do some research to see if that company is part of the stock market—does it sell stock? (The company's website will probably tell you.) The name of the company is abbreviated for its listing on the stock market. This abbreviation is the company's "symbol." Write the symbol here: _____

Now look up the symbol in the newspaper to see how much one share of the stock costs: _____

The diagram on the right shows a listing from a stock page and explains what the numbers mean.

stock	symbol	high	low	close	change	volume (00s)
Air Canada	AC	5.95	4.95	5.57	0.57	43166

Figure out how many shares you'd like to buy—how much money do you want to spend? For example, if you buy 10 shares, and each share costs $5, you'll spend $50.

Number of shares: _____   Total expense: _____

Now track how your stock does. Check the price of your stock in the newspaper each day. Use the point graph below to plot your stock over a few days or a few weeks. Does your stock go up, down, or stay the same? Have you made money, lost money, or remained even? Did you make a wise investment?

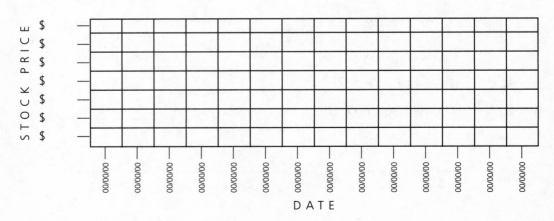

Who's Up? Who's Down?

Now that you know how to read the stock page, check the stocks of some other companies you like or are interested in. Think about big restaurant chains or entertainment companies or megastores. List the stocks on the left. Then track each stock over a few days or a few weeks. Use a different color for each stock.

- If the stock goes up, draw a line slanted upward. Keep going up if the stock continues to rise.
- If the stock goes down, draw a line slanted downward. Keeping going down if the stock continues to fall.
- If the stock remains the same, or has very little change, draw a straight line.
- If the stock fluctuates—goes up and down—draw lines to show that movement, too.

Study the lines. Which stock is doing well, staying steady, or losing money?

Stock	Day 1	Day 2	Day 3	Day 4	Day 5	Day 6	Day 7
1.							
2.							
3.							
4.							
5.							
6.							

Friendly Competition

Now play a game with your family to see who can choose a stock that earns the most money. Track the movement of your stocks on the graph below. Be sure that each family member who plays uses a different color. Have each player begin in the middle of the graph, at zero. Don't track how much your stock is worth. Instead, track how much your stock goes up or down.

Player 1: _____ Stock: _____ Color: _____

Player 2: _____ Stock: _____ Color: _____

Player 3: _____ Stock: _____ Color: _____

Player 4: _____ Stock: _____ Color: _____

	Day 1	Day 2	Day 3	Day 4	Day 5	Day 6	Day 7	Day 8	Day 9	Day 10
10										
9										
8										
7										
6										
5										
4										
3										
2										
1										
0										
-1										
-2										
-3										
-4										
-5										
-6										
-7										
-8										
-9										
-10										

Really Ripped

Think something sounds too good to be true? It just might be! People know that teens like to spend money, earn money, and just have fun. Some of the offers you may read about are true, but others are false. Read each offer below. Decide if the offer is **true** or **false**.

1. Would you like to work in the music industry? Would you like to work with top producers and discover the latest musical talents? By attending our school, you'll get all the training you need to be a big-time music producer. Tuition is only $35,000 for this two-year training. You'll earn your money back in weeks! **True?**   **False?**

2. Would you like to earn a lot of money, fast? Then try modeling! Models are some of the highest-paid workers in the world, earning thousands of dollars an hour. Join our modeling agency, and you'll soon be on your way to a lucrative modeling career. We select only a few candidates for our agency. If we select you, you'll only have to pay a nominal fee, and we'll take care of the rest! **True?**   **False?**

3. Congratulations! Because of your stellar academic record and work in the community, you have been chosen to join other exceptional students, like yourself, on a fabulous trip to our nation's capital. You'll visit the museums, the monuments, and the places where our government does business. The cost is only $5,000 for this amazing, once-in-a-lifetime opportunity! **True?**   **False?**

And the answer is . . . FALSE! These offers are not really legitimate. Here's why:

1. **The Expensive Trade School:** The best way to break into the entertainment industry is to work for the entertainment industry, not spend thousands of dollars on a trade school. Only by working with record producers and filmmakers will you actually learn about the business, firsthand.

2. **The Welcoming Modeling Agency:** As soon as you hear that a modeling agency wants your money—run! Legitimate modeling agencies do not need your money. They earn money from the clients who hire the agency's models. Do not pay an agency to represent you.

3. **The Trip of a Lifetime:** While these trips are legitimate, their prices are often exorbitant. These companies are not offering you a trip in order to be nice. They're offering you this "special" trip because they want your money! If the trip really appeals to you, research other options. You're sure to find a cheaper way of traveling.

Activities
for Young Adults

Examine Your Debts

Maybe you've just graduated from college, and you're trying to figure out what to do next. Maybe you've been working for a while, and you're trying to decide if you should move out of (or back into!) your parents' home. Transitioning from a teenager or college student to an independent adult is sometimes daunting, especially where money is concerned. So the first thing you should do is try to analyze your finances. Start by examining any money you owe. Read each question below. In the columns, write to whom you owe the money (the creditor), how much you still owe (the total balance), and the payment you make each month. If the question doesn't apply to you, write the letters n/a.

	Creditor	How Much	Monthly Payment
Do you have any student loans?			
Do you have any credit cards?			
Do you have a car loan?			
Do you owe money to your family?			
Do you owe money to anyone else?			

Examine Your Monthly Expenses

 Now you need to figure out if you have enough money to get by every month when you're out on your own. First, figure out how much money you spend every month on expenses. This work sheet does *not* include money for rent or utilities. It's strictly to find out how much money you spend *now*, each month. Complete each line of the work sheet honestly. Again, if the item doesn't apply to you, write n/a. Then add up your expenses to find the total.

Car loan or lease payment: _____

Car insurance: _____

Health insurance: _____

Student loan payment: _____

Total of all credit card payments: _____

Health club membership: _____

Cell phone service: _____

Internet service: _____

Cable service: _____

Monthly pet expenses: _____
   (dog food, cat litter, etc.)

Commuter fees: _____
   (bus, train, subway tickets
   to get to work each day) _____

Gas for your car: _____

Anything else (be honest!): _____

_____

_____

_____

TOTAL: _____

Can You Afford an Apartment?

Now you need to find out if you are financially ready to get your own apartment. Follow this three-part work sheet.

Part 1: Your Income and Expenses

How much money do your paychecks net each month?
(This is the amount after all the deductions.)   _____

How much are your monthly expenses?
(See the work sheet on page 172.)   _____

Subtract your net monthly income from your monthly
expenses. This is how much money you have left.   _____

Part 2: An Apartment and Expenses

Now do some research. Find out how much apartments or other rental properties rent for in your area. Also ask your parents or a friend to explain their utility, phone, and cable bills. Your bills might be a little bit lower (or higher), but the fees will give you an average amount.

Rent: _____

Utilities: _____

Regular phone service (not a cell phone):   _____

Cable/satellite TV (if not yet an   _____

expense from page 172):   _____

Other: _____

TOTAL: _____

Part 3: Make a Decision

- If the last number in Part 1 is larger than the last number in Part 2, then you have enough money to pay for rent and utilities on your own.

- If the last number in Part 1 is smaller than the last number in Part 2, then you **don't** have enough money to pay for rent and utilities on your own. What should you do?

Should You?
Or Shouldn't You?

One of the toughest decisions when you're starting out on your own is should you start out on your own. *Should* you get your own apartment? *Should* you rent a place with your friends? Or *should* you live with your parents? To help make your decision, write the pros and cons of each scenario on the charts below. Don't forget—your financial situation should be a consideration, too.

Should I Live with My Parents?

Pros	Cons

Should I Get My Own Apartment?

Pros	Cons

Should I Move In with Friends?

Pros	Cons

Should You Get a Roommate?

Not sure if you should get a roommate? Use this three-part questionnaire to help make your decision. Answer each question honestly.

The Money Part:

1. Do you need a roommate to help pay for expenses?

    a) yes   **b)** no   **c)** maybe

2. Do you think a roommate should split the bills 50/50?

    a) yes   **b)** no   **c)** maybe

3. Do you want your roommate's name to be on the rent/lease contract?

    a) yes   **b)** no   **c)** maybe

4. Will you check to make sure your roommate has a job and can pay the bills?

    a) yes   **b)** no   **c)** maybe

Some Advice:

1) If you answered mostly **yes** to these questions, then your decision to get a roommate is solely based on finances. You should definitely make sure your roommate can pay a fair share of the bills. If your roommate ducks out on you, you might get into financial trouble. Make sure that the roommate you choose is financially responsible and views money the same way you do.

2) If you answered mostly **no** or **maybe,** then your roommate's finances aren't as important to you. Maybe you just want a roommate because you don't want to live totally alone. That's great! If your roommate ducks out on you, you won't have to worry about how you'll pay your bills.

The Acceptance Part:

1. Will you accept a roommate who smokes?

    a) yes   **b)** no   **c)** maybe

2. Will you accept a roommate who has a dog or a cat?

    a) yes   **b)** no   **c)** maybe

3. Will you accept a roommate of the opposite sex?

  a) yes   **b)** no   **c)** maybe

4. Will you accept a roommate who comes from a background different from your own?

  a) yes   **b)** no   **c)** maybe

Some Advice:

If you answer **yes** or **no,** your decision has already been made, and that's perfectly fine. It's the **maybes** that should worry you. If you will maybe take someone who smokes, or who has a cat, you have to think how that decision will affect you. If the smoke or the cat bothers you after a week, you can't just ask your roommate to leave; you've already made a commitment. Make sure you have definite answers to these questions before you choose a roommate.

The Personality Part:

1. Do you mind if your roommate leaves dirty dishes in the sink?

  a) yes   **b)** no   **c)** maybe

2. Do you mind if your roommate has friends over to visit?

  a) yes   **b)** no   **c)** maybe

3. Do you mind if your roommate's room is a mess?

  a) yes   **b)** no   **c)** maybe

4. Do you mind if your roommate keeps different hours from yours?

  a) yes   **b)** no   **c)** maybe

Some Advice:

1) If you answered mostly **yes,** a roommate situation might not work for you. You might become too easily irritated to deal well with a roommate. You might want to consider other options.

2) If you answered mostly **no,** a roommate is probably a good idea. You understand that you and your roommate are different and will have different habits. Your roommate's different habits won't bother you. You'll probably live well with a roommate.

3) If you answered mostly **maybe,** you're mostly tolerant and won't mind your roommate's habits. Just watch out for those moments when you do become irritated.

Make a Contract

So you've decided that a roommate isn't for you and you want to move back home. Your decision not only affects you; it affects your parents, too. If you don't have younger siblings, your parents might be used to having their home all to themselves. They might be hesitant to welcome you back, afraid that you'll never leave! To make both you and your parents feel comfortable, sit down with them and work out a contract. Ask your parents what they expect of you, and assure your parents that you will live with them as a responsible adult. Below is a possible contract to get you started.

This *contract*, signed on this date _____ has been agreed upon by the following parties:

_____ (the adult child)

_____ (the parents)

The purpose of this contract is to establish the terms upon which the above-named adult child will move back into the above-named parents' home. The following terms have been discussed and agreed upon.

1. The adult child agrees to help out with chores around the home. This includes: _____

2. The adult child agrees to do his/her laundry, unless the parents ask otherwise.

3. The adult child agrees to let the parents know if he/she will be home for dinner.

4. The adult child agrees to be courteous and let the parents know his/her schedule. This does not mean that the adult child has to explain every minute of every day; but rather let parents know when he/she can be expected home so parents can make their own plans.

5. The adult child agrees to contribute to household expenses in the following ways: _____

6. The adult child agrees that this is not a permanent situation and is working toward the goal of moving out on his/her own.

7. Above all, the adult child agrees to act responsibly in his/her parents' home and to respect the fact that his/her parents have agreed to let him/her stay there.

_____
(signature of child)

_____
(signature of parents)

Working Toward Getting Out of Debt

It's so easy to run up debts while in college. Student loans, of course, are necessary to pay for school. Credit cards may also have become a necessary evil. You might have charged books, food, gas, clothes, entertainment, and other expenses. Now it's time to try to get out of debt, and one of the best ways to do so is to bump up your payments. You might have already realized that paying the minimum balance on a credit card each month does not lower the total amount you owe by very much.

This applies to your student loan, too. If you could pay off your student loan quicker, you'd have that much more money to spend—or save! Call up the financial institution through which you have your student loan, and ask how soon you can pay off your loan if you bump up your payments. Use this questionnaire to guide you.

Background:

Student loan company: _____

Phone number: _____

My account number: _____

Name of my counselor: _____

Questions to Ask:

How much do I still owe on my student loan? _____

How much interest am I paying? _____

How much of my monthly payment goes toward interest? _____

How much of my monthly payment goes toward the loan? _____

If I send an extra_____ dollars a month, how much
more quickly can I pay off my loan? _____

Do you have any other suggestions for how I might pay off
my loan more quickly?_____

_____

_____

What Does It Mean to "Live Beyond Your Means"?

Do you live beyond your means? Do you know what this phrase refers to? Your *means* are the resources, usually financial, that allow you to lead a stable and secure life. If you live *beyond* those means, then you are probably spending more money than you earn. Living beyond your means may seem like a great idea—and you may be having a great time in the process! Eventually, though, spending more than you earn will catch up with you. Take this personality quiz to see if you are in jeopardy of living beyond your means.

1. How many credit cards do you currently have?

   a) 0–1　　　　　　**b)** 2–4　　　　　　**c)** 5 +

2. Have you ever asked your credit card company to raise your limit?

   a) never　　　　**b)** only a few times　　**c)** frequently

3. How close to the limit are your credit card balances now?

   a) You currently do not owe any money, or very little money, on your credit cards.

   b) You credit cards are about halfway maxed.

   c) You're always pushing the limits on your credit cards.

4. You don't get paid for another week, and you've run out of cash. You . . .

   a) stay home and read a book or watch a movie.

   b) use your credit card and charge your expenses.

   c) use your credit card to get cash advances so you have money to spend.

5. You've maxed out your credit cards, but you really want to go with your friends to the Bahamas. You . . .

   a) tell your friends maybe next time.

   b) take the money out of the savings account you had opened to save money to buy a house.

   c) fill out the application for a new credit card, then charge the trip when the new card arrives in the mail.

6. You are with friends at dinner, and everyone is squabbling over how to pay the check. You . . .

a) agree that you should only have to pay for what you ordered.

b) agree that everyone should split the check evenly.

c) tell everyone to stop arguing and put the entire tab on your credit card.

7. Your credit card payment is due, but your checking account is short. You . . .

a) always have enough money in your checking account to pay your bills, so this would never happen.

b) pay the bill late.

c) get a cash advance from another credit card to put in your checking account so you can pay the bill.

8. Your rent is due, but your friends are going to the city for the weekend. If you pay your rent, you won't have the money to go to the city. If you go to the city, you won't have money to pay the rent. You . . .

a) pay the rent and sit home with a good book.

b) pay the rent and spend the weekend in the city with your friends—and your credit cards.

c) go to the city with the rent money; you'll worry about the rent in a few weeks.

Check Your Score

If you answered mostly A, you know how to live well within your means. You are responsible with your money, and you keep your financial priorities in mind when making decisions. You like to have a good time, but not at the expense of your finances. You are in no danger of getting into trouble with credit cards. Way to go!

If you answered mostly B, you sometimes teeter on the edge. You love to have a good time, but you also know when to say no. However, you do tend to use your credit cards a little recklessly. Your credit-card use is a habit you should try to break. Try to use your credit cards less and cancel some of the ones you have. Be careful!

If you answered mostly C, yikes! You are a credit card company's dream, but your own worst nightmare. You use credit cards recklessly and rarely think about the consequences. Your most important goal is to live for the moment, which is okay. However, the moment will soon arrive when the credit card companies and debt collectors will come knocking at your door. You are living completely beyond your means, and you need to rein in your spending habits before you get into serious trouble. Get it together—now!

Why Should You Start Saving—Now?

It may be difficult at this point in your life to find any extra money to put in savings. Your income is not that great yet, you have lots of expenses, and let's not forget having a good time. The reason to start saving as soon as possible is that someday your priorities will change. Someday you'll want to stop living in an apartment and buy a house. Someday you'll want to stop working and lie on a beach somewhere, retired.

Well, you can't do that with tons of debt and no money in the bank. And the sooner you start saving now, the more money you'll have later. The next time you're on the Internet, check out the websites of some financial institutions. Many of them will have a chart that shows how much money you will have saved if you start investing at different ages. Complete your own chart below, based on your research, with the amount of money you will have saved by the time you reach 65.

	If a 25-year-old starts saving...	If a 35-year-old starts saving...	If a 45-year-old starts saving...	If a 55-year-old starts saving...
$ 20 a month				
$ 50 a month				
$100 a month				
$200 a month				

What conclusions can you draw from this chart?

_____

_____

The only person you can depend on is yourself! Years ago, people could depend on employers to provide pensions. (A pension is money you receive from a company once you have retired.) However, many companies are starting to do away with pensions. Many retired people also depend on Social Security. But as you probably know from the news, the future of Social Security is anything but secure. Therefore, it's up to you to provide for your future financial security. You must save today for your retirement tomorrow. Once you are financially secure, you will truly know what it feels like to enjoy yourself and have a good time.

Can You Be Financially Independent?

Yes, you can! However, you need to be realistic about money. You need to have a good understanding of your spending habits and your expenses, your income and your savings. Use the following checklist to help you become financially independent. Once you can check all the items on the list, you are well on your way!

_____ I have bumped up the payments on my student loan.

_____ I do not live beyond my means.

_____ I do not have more than two credit cards.

_____ On those credit cards I do have, I do not carry much debt.

_____ I understand that credit cards can get me into big trouble.

_____ I always pay my bills on time.

_____ I have established good credit with a well-known bank or other financial institution.

_____ I always file a tax return and pay any money owed.

_____ I contribute to my 401(k) plan through my employer.

_____ I put money in savings every month.

_____ I do not pay off one credit card with another.

_____ I make some sacrifices now so that I can enjoy life when I am older.

_____ I do not rely on my parents to help me pay my bills.

_____ I understand what it means to be financially responsible.

Congratulations! You are well on your way to being financially independent!

Help on the Web

Business Cards

www.vistaprint.com   (Free business cards)

Cars

www.autotrader.com   (Available used cars)
www.carfax.com   (Vehicle history report)
www.carmax.com   (Available used cars, price comparisons)
www.consumerreports.org   (Car quality ratings)
www.edmunds.com   (Used car prices)
www.kbb.com   (Used car prices)

College

www.ed.gov   (Government guide to student loans)
www.scholarships.com   (Scholarship information)
www.fastweb.com   (Scholarship information)
www.studentaid.org   (Scholarship information)
www.fafsa.ed.gov   (Financial aid information)

Games for Kids

www.fleetkids.com   (Money games for kids)
www.lemonadegame.com   (Money games for kids)

www.moneyfactory.com/kids/start.html (Money games for kids)
www.sesamestreet.com (Money games for kids)
http://www.usmint.gov/kids (Money games for kids)

Games for Teens

www.moneyopolis.com (Money games for teens)
www.orangekids.com (Money games for teens)
www.treas.gov/kids (Money games for teens)
www.zillions.org (Money lessons for teens)

Housing Costs

www.bankrate.com (Mortgage rates and calculators)
www.hsh.com (Mortgage rates and calculators)
www.monstermoving.com (Mortgage rates and calculators)
www.realtor.com (House prices)

Investing

www.buyandhold.com (Buy individual stocks inexpensively)
www.jumpstart.org (Jump$tart Coalition for Personal Financial Literacy)
www.latimes.com/money (Investing 101 online course)
www.publicdebt.treas.gov/sav/savkids.htm (Learn about savings bonds)
www.savingsbonds.gov (U.S. Savings bonds)
www.sharebuilder.com (Buy individual stocks inexpensively)
www.smgww.org (Stock Market Game)
www.usaa.com (Info on USAA's First Start Fund)
www.vanguard.com (Info on the Vanguard STAR Fund)
www.younginvestor.com (Investor info for kids)

Long-Term Care Insurance

www.jhancock.com (John Hancock Life Insurance Co.)
www.statefarm.com (State Farm Insurance Co.)
www.usaa.com (USAA Life Insurance Co.)
www.massmutual.com (Mass Mutual Financial Group)

www.gefn.com/insurance	(GE Life and Annuity Insurance Co.)
www.metlife.com	(Metropolitan Life Insurance Co.)
www.thehartford.com	(Hartford Life Insurance Co.)
http://finance.americanexpress.com	(IDS Life Insurance Co., now part of American Express)
www.aarp.org	(AARP, guide to long-term care insurance)

Moving Back Home

www.landlord.com	(Tips and information for landlords)

Music

www.apple.com/itunes	(Pay-per-song music downloads)
www.audiostreet.net	(Free music downloads from independent artists)
www.epitonic.com	(Free music downloads from independent artists)
www.iuma.com	(Free music downloads)
www.limewire.com	(Free music downloads)
www.musicmatch.com	(Pay-per-song music downloads)
www.rhapsody.com	(Pay-per-song music downloads)
www.ubl.com	(Free music downloads from independent artists)

Parties for Kids

www.kidspartyfun.com	(See different ideas for themes and how to save big bucks on your child's big day)
www.parents.com	(See the section called "birthdays" for some great party ideas)
www.birthdayexpress.com	(Lots of great ideas and recipes for creative cakes and cupcakes)

Prom Savings

www.promadvice.com	(Saving money on the prom)

Ripoffs

www.modelingscams.org	(Avoiding modeling scams)
www.actorsource.com	(Avoiding acting scams)

Travel

www.insuremytrip.com   (Buying travel insurance)

Working and Saving

www.activeparenting.com   (Parenting education)
www.ingdirect.com   (Online savings account)

Your Parents

www.nolo.com   (Free legal information)
www.aarp.com   (Information for you and your parents)
www.aoa.gov   (The administration on aging)
www.nhtsa.dot.gov/people/injury/olddrive   (Information on older drivers)

About the Authors

Clark Howard is the host of "The Clark Howard Show," a radio talk show syndicated in more than ninety cities around the country. He is also a featured commentator on WSB-TV in Atlanta and a columnist with the *Atlanta Journal-Constitution*. Mark Meltzer is an editor at the *Atlanta Business Chronicle*. Both authors reside in Atlanta, Georgia.

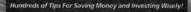